HAVE YOU WONDERED:

- What your baby will look like right after birth?

- Who should—and who shouldn't—hold your newborn?

- What you want your first hours at home with your baby to be like . . . and whether, if you want time alone *without company*, you can get it?

- When you will get your figure back?

- What the difference is between a case of the "baby blues" and real postpartum depression?

- How you can include your baby's father in the nurturing process?

- If and when you should let your baby cry?

- When you really must call your doctor *right away*?

GET THE CANDID, *ACCURATE* ANSWERS FROM A DOCTOR BASED ON HER EXPERIENCES WITH THE EXPERTS WHO REALLY KNOW—NEW MOTHERS—IN

A NEW MOTHER'S HOME COMPANION

D1532260

QUANTITY SALES

Most Dell books are available at special quantity discounts when purchased in bulk by corporations, organizations, or groups. Special imprints, messages, and excerpts can be produced to meet your needs. For more information, write to: Dell Publishing, 1540 Broadway, New York, NY 10036. Attention: Director, Special Markets.

INDIVIDUAL SALES

Are there any Dell books you want but cannot find in your local stores? If so, you can order them directly from us. You can get any Dell book currently in print. For a complete up-to-date listing of our books and information on how to order, write to: Dell Readers Service, Box DR, 1540 Broadway, New York, NY 10036.

A New Mother's

...

Home Companion

Paula Elbirt-Bender, M.D.,
with Linda Lee Small

A DELL TRADE PAPERBACK

A DELL TRADE PAPERBACK

Published by
Dell Publishing
a division of
Bantam Doubleday Dell Publishing Group, Inc.
1540 Broadway
New York, New York 10036

Library of Congress Cataloging in Publication Data
Elbirt-Bender, Paula.
    A new mother's home companion/Paula Elbirt-Bender with Linda Lee Small.
        p.   cm.
    ISBN 0-440-50663-8
    1. Infants (Newborn)—Care. 2. Mother and infant. I. Small, Linda Lee. II. Title.
    RJ253.E43   1995
    649'.122—dc20   94-20934
                                                                  CIP

Illustrated by Alice Simpson
Printed in the United States of America

Published simultaneously in Canada

March 1995

10 9 8 7 6 5 4 3 2 1

BVG

To all my mothers and children
and especially to our children

David
Shira
Melissa
and
Scotty
and
R

Acknowledgments

$\mathcal{I}$ would like to acknowledge all the mothers and fathers and their babies who shared their fears and their triumphs with me over the years. In particular I'd like to thank JB for her love, grace, and wisdom, BC for her sense of humor and courage, RB for teaching me to fight, WR and KK for smiling through it, SW for overcoming all the odds, and to JSS in memoriam for giving so much to everyone.

I especially thank my friend and colleague Ms. Naomi Siegel, M.S., for her many wisdoms and her constant support. Thank you to my partner Dr. Jacalyn H. Shafer for reviewing the manuscript and just in general for believing in me. Thank you, Pat, Carol, and Andrea, for the extra help and support you always cheerfully gave me.

Most of all, thank you, Linda, for making this project so much fun in spite of all of life's vicissitudes.

H—no words—just love.

Contents

A NEW MOTHER'S
HOME COMPANION

Introduction

*M*ore than once in my fifteen years of practice as a pediatrician a mother has called and introduced herself by saying,
"Hello, I'm a newborn mother," when of course what she
meant to say was, "I'm the mother of a newborn." But there's
truth in this slip of the tongue. In what I call the *tenth month*
—those weeks after her baby's birth—a woman is reborn into
her new role as mother. She is still a wife, friend, daughter,
daughter-in-law, but even those roles are changed forever. As
one mom said to me, "I'm not who I used to be, but I'm not
exactly who I expected to be either." I tell mothers there is life
after childbirth, but it's not the same one. The transformation
into the mother role eclipses all the others at least for a time.

Not surprisingly, new moms have questions and concerns
about caring for their babies. In the first few hours and days,
the concerns are fundamental: "Is my baby normal?" "Is she
healthy?" Then come *all* the questions about taking care of
the baby, which are asked with incredible predictability. Most
new mothers need information on how to deal with the reality
and responsibility of the small bundle of joy nestled in their
arms.

Moms frequently experience what I have come to call
"mother muddle"—a state of neediness and confusion. Nothing quite prepares mothers for this new fact of life: you are

now totally responsible for another human being. New mothers need to understand what has happened to them and what will happen to them in the weeks to come.

New mothers also have many questions about caring for themselves. When I do the routine two-week checkup of the baby, I always ask the mother, "How are *you?*" And they tell me. (As the mother of three children, I understand what they are going through.) Often after we've met, I get calls from these same mothers with questions not only about their babies, but more commonly, they ask me about concerns they have about themselves as well. ("When I pass the mirror, I don't recognize myself" or "I know I'm supposed to be happy, but all I do is cry" or "I feel so dumb. I thought breast-feeding was supposed to be so easy.") They ask, "Should I be calling *you?*" and I invariably answer, "Who else would you call?" After an intense nine-month relationship, their obstetrician/gynecologist has often faded from the picture, and the pediatrician is now clearly in the spotlight. You could say that pediatricians really have two "patients": mother and baby. We cannot separate the two. I wouldn't want to.

A New Mother's Home Companion will track the journey both mother and child embark upon after birth and through the first three months. Although this book will try to address all the myriad questions I have been asked, it should be used along with your naturally good instincts. I tell "my parents," no one knows your baby as well as you do. Use what advice feels right; what doesn't, discard.

Over the years, I have conducted "new mothers' groups"—after-hours sessions just for moms. I began these groups as a "cure" for a common affliction: new mothers are often isolated and alone. Mothers don't just need information. They ache for reassurance—to hear that what they are experiencing is being experienced by other mothers as well. I've tried to gather my mothers together, not in one room, but into this book. Their voices, both their victories and laments, fill *A New Mother's Home Companion*.

This book will help promote what I call the 3 C's—competence, confidence, and comfort. My objective always is to help "raise" happy moms, because inevitably happy moms produce happy babies.

PART I:
THE HOSPITAL EXPERIENCE

CHAPTER *1*

. . . .

The Newborn Baby

*C*ongratulations! You have finally given birth. After nine months of daydreaming and planning, you have reached that magic moment—a moment which has to be experienced to be understood. No one can really describe what it *feels* like when a newborn baby emerges into this world. It's miraculous, plain and simple.

Don't be surprised if time just seems to stand still and images are distorted—but just momentarily.

THE DELIVERY ROOM EXPERIENCE

The baby emerges with a final push. In a vaginal delivery what you see first is a lot of bloody fluid. Very soon afterward you will see your glistening, sparkling, shiny wet baby being slid up and over your pelvis and onto your belly. She is still attached to the winding umbilical cord emerging from between your legs. As she is handed up to you, the cord lengthens along with her. Most mothers are so relieved and dazzled by the baby that they don't pay much attention to the cord or, for that matter, to most of what is happening at their pelvis. In a cesarean section, if you are awake (and the majority of women are), the baby will be lifted up into the air still attached to the cord and placed in your arms at your chest. (In emergency C-sections, the baby will first be quickly examined and then shown to you when everything is determined to be "okay.")

At the moment of birth you will hear someone announce the exact time of birth, but you won't see a nurse turn the baby upside down and slap her as in old movies.

When the baby's head first appears or just when the baby is put on your stomach, you will probably hear odd "gurgling" noises as the doctors and nurses suction from your baby's mouth and nose the amniotic fluid she swallowed in her passage through the birth canal. (Amniotic fluid is the clear pinkish liquid in which the baby floated while in utero.) Some babies, particularly in vaginal deliveries, need extra suctioning, so you may hear slurping sounds, a lot like a vacuum cleaner makes, as the nurse uses a flexible tube in the baby's mouth to suction out amniotic fluid and blood to help your baby breathe more easily.

Once the baby is brought to your chest, you may feel a tugging on your uterus which can be painful, but at this moment it seems largely irrelevant when compared to the precious baby in your arms.

Babies get cold quickly. The nurses will put little blankets over the baby while she is still connected to you by the umbilical cord. Unless you have prearranged with your obstetrician to have your partner participate in the cutting of the cord, the doctor will snip and clamp it with a special plastic device. Instead of a clamp, some hospitals use "triple-dye"—a chemical which dries up the cord—and the cord will look as if it's been dyed purple. You may see some of what's going on at your pelvis and feel discomfort or even sharp pain while the placenta (the so-called afterbirth) is coming out, but again your focus will still be on your newborn.

Most parents confide that the newborn looked less than beautiful but actually quite wrinkled and purple—and that was just fine! There is no other moment to rival this one. It's special even for the staff in the delivery room. When I was a pediatric resident, I was often in the delivery room, and never saw anyone connected with a birth respond casually to this truly blessed event. This is actually the bonding period researchers referred to when they originally described the need for mothers to bond with their babies. (Now we realize this moment is not indispensable and no harm is done for those moms who miss this because of medical necessity.) Some babies alternately cry and then calm in your arms. This is a wonderful opportunity to help the baby to suck on your breast or finger: if you place the newborn at your nipple, she will usually suck even though there is *no* milk. (In fact, she may not suck again this calmly until many hours later.)

This magic period actually lasts for just a few minutes, which is usually long enough. As exhaustion sets in, especially in your arms and legs, a nurse will take your baby just a few feet away and put her on a warmer. This is a specially built infant-sized bed where heat lamps radiate down from the top. A small probe, which doesn't hurt or burn, will be taped to your baby's body to monitor her temperature so that the warmer is always at the correct setting.

Your natural instinct will be to follow the baby. If you turn and look to your side, you may see the nurse cleaning and drying her on the warmer. Then you'll see the nurse with a stethoscope listening intently to the baby's chest, flicking the baby's heels, picking up her arms and letting them drop in what appears to you to be a rather abrupt manner. It's all routine. The nurse is making a determination of your baby's Apgar score.

The Apgar test is your baby's first test. Apgar scores are universally given at one minute, five minutes, and in some cases ten minutes to evaluate or measure the baby in five areas: respiration, heart rate, muscle tone, reflexes, and color. The baby isn't put through any specific tests but rather is observed, and is given a 0, 1, or 2 in each area. In the best circumstances the total score would be 10 (which is where the expression "a perfect 10" originally came from). Rarely if ever can a baby get a 10 at the first minute of life, because they are "less than pink" at birth. (Variations in color from slightly pale to rosy are perfectly normal.) Generally speaking you are not told the score, unless you ask, but typically a healthy baby gets at least a 7. C-section babies tend to have slightly higher Apgar scores, because they don't have much difficulty coming out and their color is usually better.

APGAR TABLE			
SIGN	**POINTS**		
	0	1	2
Appearance (color)*	Pale or blue	Body pink, extremities blue	Pink
Pulse (heartbeat)	Not detectable	Below 100	Over 100
Grimace (reflex irritability)	No response to stimulation	Grimace	Lusty cry
Activity (muscle tone)	Flaccid (no or weak activity)	Some movement of extremities	A lot of activity
Respiration (breathing)	None	Slow, irregular	Good (crying)

*In nonwhite children, color of mucous membranes of mouth, of the whites of the eyes, of lips, palms, hands, and soles of feet will be examined.

You will also see the nurse putting ointment in the eyes to protect the baby from a variety of infections that could occur during the birth process. You may also hear the baby cry as she is given a shot of vitamin K in her thigh to prevent a rare cause of bleeding in newborns. In some hospitals the baby is also given a shot of penicillin to prevent a specific type of infection caused by vaginal bacteria.

In the delivery room your baby will be registered and a tag

put on her ankle. The baby will be footprinted and you will be fingerprinted right onto the birth certificate, so that for all time it's clear that you are this baby's mommy.

The nurses will wrap up the baby after the five-minute Apgar and give you back your dried, tested, registered, and quite wonderful baby. This is the perfect moment to meet your baby. This is often when I see new mothers peek carefully under the blankets—almost as if they are afraid to mess them up. The need to count fingers and toes and really *look* at this baby is overwhelming. Both parents will start to exclaim: "Oh my God, he looks just like . . ." or *"Who* does he look like?" Parents will joyfully respond when they see what they "like": "Oh, look, he has beautiful blue eyes," and occasionally also be taken aback at what appears to be less than perfect: "What's this bruise, this bump, this red mark?" Most of these birthmarks are just that—the result of the process of birth, and fade away in just a matter of hours. (More about these marks later.)

After you've held and examined this nicely wrapped baby (who may now be slightly unwrapped by you), there will come a time—anywhere from fifteen minutes to an hour and a half later—when the nurses take the baby to the nursery and you to the recovery room. (In some hospitals the baby will be wheeled with you to the recovery room and *then* taken to the nursery.) You may feel a little sad to let her go so soon or you might just be relieved. The clerk in the delivery room will call up to the nursery and announce: "Baby coming up."

SCENE 2: THE NURSERY

Your baby is now in the nursery—a glass-enclosed room where there is a lot of contact between the staff and the babies. Your baby is the "new kid on the nursery block," which alerts the staff to keep an eye on her. A nurse will completely unwrap the baby and put her on the scale to determine her birth weight. Then her measurements will be taken: length and size of head, chest, and abdomen. She will be placed once again on a warmer, where she will be observed naked for the next two to three hours.

While she is on the warmer, her temperature will again be monitored by a probe which is attached to her by tape. The nurse will do a full examination of the baby, listening to the heart and making sure the lungs are clear. (I often see the daddy outside the nursery window watching all the goings-on.)

During this period, the baby often appears to be very calm and peaceful. If you could peek into the nursery, you would see her lying very quietly making some smooth movements and occasionally jerky ones—very similar to what she was like in the womb. She may even curl into a fetal position. If you've had anesthesia, the baby has gotten some of it too through the umbilical cord and could be a little groggy. Your baby needs to slowly recover from the experience of childbirth. (I'm often reminded of the "talking" newborn in the movie *Look Who's Talking* who, immediately after birth, keeps repeating: "Put me back.")

After a few hours of observation, the baby will be dressed in hospital clothing. Most hospitals use loosely cuffed T-shirts with strings or snaps, a baby diaper, and a little "sock hat" on her head to keep her warm: the head is such a large part of her body that a lot of heat can be lost through it. If the baby has long nails, which is the case for many postmature babies (those babies who were born after forty weeks of gestation), then she will be dressed in a long-sleeved T-shirt which has cuffs that can be pulled down over her fingers so that she can't scratch herself. To prevent the accidental nipping of the skin, nurses are instructed to leave the nails unclipped. Finally the baby will be wrapped in a square cotton swaddling blanket. It's been observed that babies are usually much happier when they are swaddled—that is, wrapped in snug-fitting clothes and blanket. (Remember, your baby has been in pretty tight quarters for the last nine months.) The reason behind swaddling is that babies are subject to the Moro or startle reflex, which causes their limbs to flail out and back at random times. They have no control over this neurological event, which momentarily upsets them. It can be somewhat reduced by swaddling.

Your baby is almost ready for the journey to your room. She will be put into a crib with a label attached to it listing vital information—such as her last name, your name, time of birth, and birth weight. The nurse keeps track of events as they happen to your baby, such as "first urination" and "first stools," often by recording them on the chart on the crib.

GETTING TO KNOW YOUR NEWBORN

Once your baby has been brought to your room and the distractions of the delivery room are gone, it is the perfect opportunity for the two of you to get to know each other. Take a moment to undress your baby completely and just look at her, a new little person in her own right.

Babies change a great deal the first few days. The baby handed to you on the delivery table may in fact look very little like the one you see now only a few hours later. Her head may still be very pointy, odd, or misshapen, but less so than at birth. If you had a C-section, she will look more like what you expected, because she hasn't traveled through the vaginal canal. (Her face is less flattened and the head is rounder.) A four-hour-old baby, however, rarely resembles those perfect infants who appear on detergent boxes and baby formula cans.

I tell all new mothers: *Think of your newborn as a work in progress.* Babies are unfinished from their GI tract to the muscular system. Few of the many functions of the body are working at complete capacity yet. There is a lot of fine tuning which will develop with usage. (For example, the signals from the brain which tell the two eyes to focus together on the same thing aren't coordinated yet, so newborns are often described as "cockeyed.") Control of body temperature is uneven, so she may easily overheat or chill. Everything inside your baby is developing in fits and starts. You could say that what you are holding is just a *sketch* of your baby—the entire picture will be slowly and brightly colored in.

As you look at her, you will notice that the baby's body is still in a fetal position. The newborn maintains this position for many weeks after birth. It serves a purpose: Babies aren't born with the best temperature regulation, and this position helps keep the warmth closer to their bodies. Her shoulders are hunched up, her arms are flexed, and her hands are fisted. If the baby was born in a breech position, and her buttocks emerged first, you may find her sucking on her toes for a few days. In the womb, her hips were flexed and her knees were held high up on her chest. As her ability to move develops and her body grows, she will gradually begin to unfold out of these positions.

You may notice lots of little marks and blemishes. I like to think of it this way: Your baby is like a little prizefighter. She's survived for nine months underwater and then gone "ten rounds" through the birth canal. She's emerged the "winner" with all the bumps and bruises to prove it. She may have a little scab on her head from the fetal monitor. She may have pimples on her body *(Erythema toxicum)* as a result of your hormones, and her fingers and toes may be a little purple. (Babies are often accused of looking like little old men—that's because there are a lot of wrinkles and folds all over them as the result of having soaked in an amniotic fluid bath for nine months.)

She may, in fact, have a variety of birth-related marks. At the base of the neck you may see "stork" bites, so named because that is supposedly where the stork carries the baby with its beak! The scientific name is *Nevus flameus*, which simply means "red mark" and is a collection of tiny blood vessels under the skin. They may also be present between the eyebrows, under the nostrils, or on the eyelids. These irregularly shaped marks are flat and have no special texture. There may also be a bluish discoloration at the base of the spine or over the buttocks. No one knows *why* any of these marks appear, but almost universally they fade by the time the baby celebrates her first birthday.

FROM HEAD TO TOE: INSIDE AND OUT

Some babies are born with a lot of *hair*, and others are almost bald at birth. Babies who have dark hair on their heads tend to have body hair as well which covers their shoulders, the small of their back, maybe the forehead, and tips of their ears. Your baby will not grow into a gorilla or transform at night into a tiny werewolf—most of this hair will gradually fall off. The texture of the fine "primary" hair will change, but at first it's scattered unevenly, and may even stick straight up. Even bald babies have some fuzz.

- The *head* makes up about one third of the surface area and is almost huge in relation to the rest of a baby's body. Babies appear to have large foreheads because they have so little hair. Everybody has heard about the "soft" spot, or fontanelle, but there are actually two soft spots. One is right smack at the top of the head, and the second, smaller one is slightly toward the back. Although perfectly normal, this second one is the cause of some phone calls to me in the middle of the night. So that the skull can accommodate the baby's brain as it grows, the head is made up of six overlapping flat bones. As needed, these bones slide apart to give the growing brain more room. Run your hand gently over her head and you'll feel many irregularities or ridges. These are all normal and are the edges of these skull bones as they override each other.
- The *eyes* may cross. Most are a blue-gray color, which will change over six months.
- The *lids* are puffy and don't stay open long.
- The *eyebrows and lashes* are faint and not easy to see.
- The *ears* may appear not to match. One may be curled forward and one back.

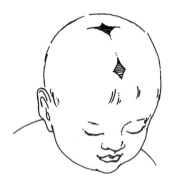

The newborn's head has two small openings called fontanelles. The smaller posterior fontanelle closes soon after birth, while the anterior one, known as the "soft spot," is open into the second year of life.

- The *nose* has a flat, wide bridge.
- The inside of the *mouth* has ridges and may have several white bumps along the gumline and palate.
- The *cheeks* are puffy and very strong.
- The *skin* will begin to exfoliate, flake. It is often driest at the ankles and wrists.
- The *nipples* may be hard and knobby and may even leak a clear fluid.
- The *belly button* has a one- or two-inch-long yellowish, plastic-looking stump, the decaying umbilical cord.
- The *hands and feet* may be purplish in color and wrinkled.
- The *nails* are long, thin, transparent, and often quite sharp.
- The *genitalia* of babies are often enlarged by the pressure on them during a vaginal birth and the large quantity of hormones transferred from the mother. The vulva and la-

bia in girls and the scrotum in boys all appear quite large in comparison to the rest of the body. Your new daughter may have a vaginal discharge, which is quite normal. In most boys, when the scrotum is relaxed, you can see and feel two marble-sized testicles. Some boys are born with one or both testicles not yet in the scrotum. (Often this condition resolves within a year. The pediatrician should discuss this with you.) The penis has a covering of skin, known as the foreskin, which extends over the top of the penis and narrows a bit—a little like a sock that is pulled too long on a foot. If the penis is left uncircumcised, this foreskin will remain. If the baby is circumcised, the fore-skin will be removed.

WHAT CAN MY BABY DO?

A lot of research has been done trying to figure out just what a newborn is capable of. The noted child researcher Dr. Michael Lewis, and his teams, have thousands of hours of tapes of new babies. His aim is to document what a baby can do. It is clear from the research that rather than being a blank slate which needs to be filled in with information, a baby already has a considerable repertoire of skills. All her senses are operating—she can smell; taste (babies reject formula they don't like, and although they are toothless, we know they are born with a "sweet tooth"); feel (in fact, they have a highly developed sense of touch and will often soothe when you hold them. And we know they can feel pain); hear; and see.

What Lewis and other researchers such as Dr. Stanley Greenspan have discovered is that even newborns try to com-municate with us. Babies are really half of a communicating team from the moment of birth. Your daughter can "talk" to you if only you know how to translate. For instance, it's been noted that almost from birth, a baby will look to catch your eye. She can't focus on you for long, and she can only see well about a foot or so away; but if you smile when she catches your eye, she will catch your eye for longer periods. You may even be rewarded with a rudimentary smile. It won't be a full-blown grin, of course, but the corners of her mouth will curl up a little bit. (Try it. Smile repeatedly when she looks at you.) A newborn can *see* best at about six to twelve inches away—the rest is fuzzy. She blinks her eyes open and shut as you get closer to her and flutters her eyelids when you withdraw.

Your baby *can make sounds.* She can make high- and low-pitched cries, but she can't modulate very well. Mostly she makes soft squeaks, tweaks, and grunts—sounds which are produced in the voice box but which seem to come from deep within her chest.

Babies can *hear* at birth but they don't always respond to sounds. (Don't test your baby's hearing by clapping your hands around her head—her lack of an immediate response may disappoint or even alarm you.) Babies have the ability to selectively inhibit noises: sometimes they respond, even in their sleep to soft noises; and sometimes they don't respond to loud ones even when they are awake. They do seem to have a preference for soft sounds—possibly because for nine months they listened to the world through several layers of your body—and repetitious sounds, perhaps reminiscent of the sound of your heartbeat.

In terms of *motor skills*, you will see that he can move his arms, kick his feet, cry, blink his eyes, open and close his mouth, suck, and grasp—he may even tug on your hair or your finger. He can move his head around, but he doesn't have strong neck muscle control yet—so he can lift it only briefly. The head appears to be in a lot of motion as he twists it from side to side. If you put the baby on your shoulders, he may stretch his neck out momentarily and seem to be craning.

A PARTIAL LIST OF THE NEWBORN'S REFLEXES

NAME	TO ELICIT	BABY'S MOVEMENTS	POSSIBLE USE TO BABY
Moro, or startle	Suddenly change position, dropping baby's head backward, or make a loud noise next to baby	Throws out arms and legs, then pulls them back convulsively	Attempt to grab mother for protection, comfort
Root	Touch cheek or area around mouth	Turns head toward stimulus	Nursing aid
Suck	Touch mucous membranes inside mouth	Sucks on object	Nursing aid
Grasp	Touch palm of hand or sole of foot	Closes hand or curls foot	To hold mother while feeding, being carried
Babinski	Stroke outside of sole of foot	Large toe curls up	Unknown
Hand to mouth	Stroke cheek *or* palm	Turns head toward stroke, bends arms up, and brings hand to mouth; mouth opens and sucks	Feeding aid; may help to clear baby's air passage
—	Shine bright light in eyes	Closes eyes	Protects eyes
Blink	Clap hands	Eyes close	Protects eyes
—	Cover mouth	Turns head away and flails arms	Prevents smothering
—	Stroke leg	Other leg crosses and pushes object away	Protection
Withdrawal	Give baby a painful stimulus	Baby withdraws	Protects body
—	Place baby on belly	Holds head up, then turns	Prevents smothering

NAME	TO ELICIT	BABY'S MOVEMENTS	POSSIBLE USE TO BABY
TNR (tonic neck reflex)	Turn baby's head to side	Whole body arches away, arm and leg move to "fencing" position	Helps in birth
Step	Stand baby	Baby walks	Practice walking movements

Some of baby's movements are out of his control and governed by reflexes: his "strings" are being pulled by Mother Nature. If you want to bring your baby's mouth into a sucking mode, stroke the side of the face near the mouth and he will begin to purse his mouth as if to suck. This "rooting" reflex is helpful in getting him to the nipple. The whole upper body may jerk (the "Moro," or "startle," reflex)—the arms and fingers may flail outward and then return toward the body and relax. The baby is not nervous, but it often looks that way. (If your baby turns his head to the left, his left arm will extend and his right arm flexes up to his head. This posture, officially known as "tonic neck reflex," is also called the "fencer's stance" because that's just what it looks like!) These are all normal neurological reflexes. Your baby's movements will gradually become more deliberate; after the first few months he'll be able to coordinate the use of parts of his body which now move fitfully or in response to these reflexes.

Your baby breathes irregularly—it could be quickly for a period of fifteen seconds, followed by a slow shallow period of five to ten seconds. The normal breathing pattern for baby in the first twenty-four hours is about three or four times the rate of adults. (Even his heart rate is naturally almost twice yours but will slow down in about two months.) Newborns periodically cough and sneeze in order to keep their airway clear.

BABY CARE

The baby will be examined by a pediatrician within twenty-four hours of birth. The doctor will then visit you on a daily basis after seeing the baby and answer any questions or concerns you may have. For example, if you have a boy, you have to decide whether to have him circumcised. (See Box.) Sometimes the doctor will share some of his own philosophy about baby care with you. (You may have chosen your pediatrician before the baby's birth, but if not your obstetrician will assign one to your baby for the hospital stay.)

CIRCUMCISION

Circumcision is done in the hospital, usually on the second or third day. You must give your permission in writing in order to have it done. In Judaism, it is often done at home on the eighth day by a person trained in the religious rituals of circumcision.

This has become a controversial issue, but it is currently more "fashionable" to circumcise boys. (In some urban centers as many as 70 percent of all infant boys are circumcised.) There are some health benefits associated with being circumcised. Some research shows that circumcision may reduce the incidence of urinary tract infections and may even reduce the incidence of cancer of the penis and cervical cancer in his future partners.

On the other hand, there are risks associated with any operative procedure—there is always a small risk of bleeding or infection—and you are making a decision for your baby which is lifelong. There is also the issue of pain. (The logical assumption is that babies *do* feel pain much as adults do. Anybody who ever accidentally hurt a baby knows that by the baby's instant cry.) It is difficult to give anesthesia around the penis without creating risks just from doing so, so no pain medication is given—and alternate means of pain relief are currently being sought.

The procedure is routinely performed by the obstetrician, who is a surgeon, and not by a pediatrician. The foreskin, which is the long tube of skin that covers the head of the penis, is first carefully stretched by the obstetrician and separated from the head of the penis and removed with a scalpel. A clamp is left on the cut end for a few minutes so that there is no need for stitches and so that when the clamp is removed the bleeding has already stopped.

After circumcision, your baby may go home with you only after he has urinated. In general, the circumcised penis requires very little aftercare. Usually a strip of gauze saturated with Vaseline is wrapped around the head of the penis so that it doesn't stick to the wound as it heals. Usually the gauze falls off after twenty-four hours; if not, you will be advised to carefully remove it. After that, apply more Vaseline to either a gauze pad or directly onto the inside of the diaper where it will come in contact with the penis while it completely heals over the next two to four days. This will protect the penis from rubbing against a dry surface. (Note: The head of a circumcised penis often has a purple-blue color, which is normal. An uncircumcised penis is also bluish at the tip, but you don't see it because the foreskin covers it.) While the circumcision is healing, the tissue around where the cut was made may become yellow-green in color, and might easily be mistaken for infected skin. It's normal and to be expected.

The nurses, too, will be regularly checking on and taking care of your baby—doing some of the routine care (diapering, bathing, feeding) that will be taken over by you very soon. Generally the baby resides in the nursery and visits you every four hours.

Your newborn will be experiencing many "firsts" in her young life.

For at least four hours after her birth, the baby will be on the warmer being observed and will not be fed anything. For their *first feed* and sometimes the second feed as well, all babies are routinely given water. Generally it's plain sterile water followed by glucose water. At birth there is sometimes a dramatic decrease in baby's glucose level. You may not like the idea of your baby getting sugar water (it sounds as if your child is being given Kool-Aid), but glucose is part of what naturally runs through our veins. (As a matter of fact, in some cultures, shortly after birth, the midwife will prepare a solution using whatever sugar source is on hand—maybe beet sugar—and mix it with boiled water and then use some kind of sponge to squeeze it directly into the baby's mouth. This is done to prevent hypoglycemic tremors.)

At the end of the first day or the next day, your baby will get her *first bath*. This is often not done in front of you, unless the baby is rooming-in with you (see Chapter 2), and is usually done by a nurse. A basin is filled with warm soapy water, and the baby is placed in the tub. The nurse will vigorously wash the baby from top to bottom with a washcloth. During this first bath the nurse will wipe off what is left of the vernix— that is, the white sticky material which is protective of the baby in utero. Vernix seems to be a natural moisturizer and protects the skin from the fluid the baby has been floating in. It may also have antibacterial properties, which is why the vernix is not completely wiped off in the delivery room. After the baby is cleaned, she is taken to a second basin containing fresh water or over to a big sink in the nursery to be rinsed off. She will get a bath every day that she is in the nursery.

The nurse will pay special attention to your baby's eyes. You will recall that ointment is put in her eyes at birth to prevent infection, but this ointment can cause the lids to become puffy and she may even develop an eye discharge. The nurses will soon wipe this material off the eyes and use warm water to keep the eyes clean and clear.

Before you go home, the plastic clamp that was put on your baby's cord in the delivery room will be removed. The one-inch dry, twisted stump which remains will fall off in one to two weeks.

During the baby's stay she will also be subjected to a variety of *tests*. There are a series of very routine blood tests, for example, which are done on your baby in most hospitals. In addition, some states require free screening tests which look for metabolic disorders that are detectable and treatable in newborns. These tests are done by the nurse or technician by drawing blood from the baby's heel—this is why you may see a Band-Aid there on your baby. You can remove the Band-Aid after an hour or so.

One routine test is to measure the bilirubin level which, if elevated, is a sign of jaundice. (Bilirubin is a yellow substance produced by the body when breaking down red blood cells.)

JAUNDICE

About one third of *all* newborns develop a yellow tinge to their skin by the third day of life. Sometimes doctors can predict which babies are more likely to develop jaundice by knowing your blood type and the baby's blood type. (In the delivery room blood is routinely taken from the umbilical cord: A test called a Coombs is done which determines whether your blood and your baby's blood antibodies are compatible. If the results are positive, then it means your blood and the baby's are incompatible and jaundice is more likely.) When your blood and your baby's pass each other in utero, some of your antibodies pass to the baby; if your blood types are not compatible, a reaction may occur that causes the red blood cells to break and release a substance called bilirubin. If the baby's liver is overwhelmed with a lot of this substance, jaundice occurs because bilirubin is yellow and it accumulates in the skin.

Don't be alarmed if you are told your baby is a little jaundiced. It's *not* a disease. The nurses will draw small samples of blood from your baby's heel two or three times a day. Usually no treatment is necessary unless the bilirubin is over 15 milligrams per deciliter of blood (15 mg/dl). Sometimes all that's needed is more frequent monitoring.

Although jaundice is not remedied by giving excess amounts of water, the doctor may ask you to nurse and feed the baby more often, hoping bowel movements will soon follow so that some of the bilirubin can be excreted that way.

The treatment for jaundice is based on the fact that a certain wavelength of light which is found naturally in sunlight can help to eliminate bilirubin from the skin by breaking it down so it can excreted in the urine and feces. Unfortunately, real sunlight also has ultraviolet radiation and can burn the baby.

To treat jaundice we use "sunlight" created by special artificial lights that break down the bilirubin so that the baby's liver doesn't have to do all the work.

For these treatments the baby is undressed except for a minidiaper so that almost the entire body is available for exposure to the light. She is placed in an incubator which has clear plastic sides so that the special light can shine through. Her eyes are covered so that the light won't annoy her. Babies stay in their little "suntan parlor" except for feedings so they can spend the maximum time under these lights. The nurses will come in and turn the baby from front to back and then later from back to front. When you look in, it does appear that your baby is happily sunbathing. For reasons which are not clear, babies seem to be very calm under the lights and rarely cry. It could be because of the warmth. This is baby's home until the bilirubin is at an acceptable level—usually under 15.

Babies with jaundice are often kept in the hospital an extra day or two because most cases don't begin until the third day. It takes that long for the bilirubin to collect in the skin. It's also possible that jaundice may not be discovered until after discharge, but this will easily be handled by your pediatrician. If your baby appears yellow anytime before her two-week checkup, call the doctor.

The baby is in a rapid phase of change these first hours and days. I would strongly advise you to cherish these early moments, and abandon, whenever possible, preconceived notions about babies. Slow down the clock, and watch as the miraculous little person unfolds before you. Watch while your newborn moves in her own gentle dance. Both of you have a lifetime to learn all her steps. Take pictures of her daily, and label them; you will be absolutely amazed at her transformation in the days and weeks to come.

CHAPTER 2

The "Newborn" Mother: The Hospital Stay

*W*ithin a short period of time after entering the delivery room, you have gone from being a pregnant woman to being a mother. Congratulations again! You remain in the delivery room for about another fifteen or twenty minutes until you have also delivered the "afterbirth" (actually the placenta). Then the doctor either stitches you up if you've had an episiotomy (an incision made by the doctor next to the vagina to allow room for the baby to emerge) or closes the incisions if you've had a cesarean section.

THE RECOVERY ROOM

Soon you will be helped onto a bed and wheeled to the recovery room. In some hospitals the baby, all cleaned up and wrapped in a blanket, will be placed in your arms and wheeled along with you. Your partner is probably right beside you as well. After delivery all women are taken to a recovery room which is set aside solely for this purpose. Usually there are curtains which can be pulled around each bed for privacy.

If you've had anesthesia, it's beginning to wear off so you are probably experiencing some pain. Often during the pushing phase of delivery the vaginal area becomes numb so that pain is minimal. This appears to be nature's way of ensuring that you continue to push hard until the baby emerges. You will start to feel pain around the vaginal opening and from any stitches that you may have needed. Nurses will come in periodically to check on you. When the nurse comes in, ask for ice packs, which will help stop both the pain and the bleeding; she may offer you pain relief medication such as Tylenol as well. (If you have had your baby with you, she will soon be taken away to the nursery.)

A nurse will come in and press on your abdomen to check that your uterus is contracting and to change the pads you are lying on, which may get blood-soaked. She will also take your vital signs (temperature, blood pressure, etc.). If you feel you have to urinate, ask the nurse to bring you a bedpan—you will probably not be steady enough to walk to the bathroom. Don't worry about having a bowel movement. You usually won't have one for a couple of days until your bowel recuperates from labor.

During this time you may feel hungry—it probably has been a very long time since you've eaten. Make sure your partner brings you a sandwich if you didn't pack one. I've seen many brand-new moms eagerly downing tuna fish sandwiches washed down with a paper cupful of bubbly c! ampagne. Although your partner can stay with you in the recovery room, fathers often scurry out to the telephone to call relatives and friends with the news. (Alas, there are no phones at your recovery room bedside.) He may even run up to the nursery to find out what the baby weighs and to peek through the glass in hopes of seeing the baby again.

Many new mothers suddenly feel quite alone. Your family is not allowed into the recovery room, although they may well be sitting in the waiting room. It's not uncommon for women to confide in me they feel a little "peculiar." You are experiencing some pain and you have no idea how bad it may get. You just had a baby, but you don't have her with you. You just became a mother, but where is the father? Hopefully your husband will rejoin you shortly and share some news about the baby.

You will be very eager to reunite with your baby. It's important that you understand that how long you remain in the recovery room usually has very little to do with you, and everything to do with *when* you delivered and if your room is ready. Hospitals are, in fact, run a little bit like hotels, with checkout time about noon. It takes housekeeping another hour or more to make up the room. In a busy hospital, if you delivered anytime after midnight you may not get to your room until 2 P.M. the next day!

You will be both relieved and excited when you are wheeled, still in your bed, to the maternity/nursery floor. If flowers or balloons have already arrived for you, they may be next to you or tied to the rail of your bed. You will stop at the front desk of the maternity floor to check in and then you will be wheeled to your room.

YOUR ROOM

If you've gone on a tour of the maternity floor while you were pregnant, you will have a better sense of what to expect in the way of accommodations. Most rooms have very little furnishings: a bed which has side rails; a bedside table with a telephone; a rolling cart where food is served; a television; a lamp; and a single chair which is magically supposed to accommodate all your visitors. Semiprivate rooms often have a bathroom with a shower, although sometimes the shower is down the hall.

Unless you have made arrangements for a private room, you will share your room with another woman who usually will be another new mother. Your roommate may, instead, be a pregnant woman who has been put on bed rest for a variety of reasons.

Shortly after your arrival a nurse will come into the room and take your vital signs again. She will show you how to most comfortably get up and down from bed. In some hospitals a nurse will give you a "doughnut," or a cushion to sit on which provides some relief from the swelling in your vaginal area. When you want to sit up: lift your knees, tuck the doughnut underneath your behind; put another pillow under your thighs; lean back on your elbows; and then put your legs over the side of the bed and sit up. (This *sounds* hard to do and sometimes it is, but it quickly gets easier.)

In most hospitals you will be offered the option of *rooming-in*—that is, having your baby remain in the room with you all the time. When you are making your decision, keep in mind how brief your stay is likely to be. Hospital stays used to be seven days; now it is commonly two days for a vaginal delivery, but it could be as little as thirty-six hours! (If you deliver the baby eleven-thirty on Monday night, you will probably be discharged and gone by noon on Wednesday.) If you've had a cesarean section, you may be discharged as early as the fourth day.

If you do chose rooming-in, an isolette (a clear plastic box with baby bedding inside) is brought to your room along with a plastic bassinet. Instead of your baby going back to the nursery when you have visitors, the baby goes into the isolette and remains in your room for all to see. That's strictly a matter of hospital policy, and is based on the desire to prevent the spread of germs from your visitors to your newborn.

The advantage to rooming-in is that you really begin to be your baby's caretaker immediately: everything this baby does, you see. (If you room-in, you need either a private room *or* the half of the semiprivate room that is by the window so that you are not being bothered by other people's visitors. Most hospitals try to put two rooming-in mothers in the same room whenever possible.) The major disadvantage is that you are probably exhausted, and could use some rest. If you can, wait to make the decision of whether or not to room-in until after the experience of delivery.

There will be times when the choice is *not* yours but governed by hospital policy. For example, you won't be offered rooming-in if you've had a C-section. Even if *you* think you are physically up to it, the hospital can't rely on you, after this major operation, to carry the baby safely in and out of the bassinet.

Remember that you don't have to be a rooming-in mother to be a *real* mother. Even if you have not chosen rooming-in, you *can* choose to have the baby with you practically all the time. (The exception is during visiting hours, when the baby will have to be returned to the nursery.) I playfully tell mothers: Ask and you shall receive—your baby. This is your baby; possession and ownership reside with you.

THE REUNION

After a few hours, the nurse will roll the clear plastic crib on wheels, with your baby in it, into your room. She will ask you to read your identification number from your wristband. You may be impatient and say, "I know my baby," but be sure your numbers do match.

After identification, the nurse usually just leaves. This is the first time you two are absolutely alone—unless your partner is still with you. There are as many possible reactions at this first mother-and-baby reunion as there are mothers and babies. Some women feel frightened or even disconnected. You may not immediately fall in love with the bundle in your arms. Or you may be unprepared for the rush of love you instantly feel.

The predictable pattern is for you to feel very protective of your newborn and in fact for the newborn to calm only to your particular touch. There will be a flood of emotions. Typically you are bombarded with warm loving feelings, but you may also be a little put off or even afraid of the newborn. Some of the most anxiety-ridden mothers I've encountered were those who felt that these negative feelings were abnormal. In fact, it's all quite natural.

Your baby may be in a deep, deep sleep, or she may be awake and kicking, though this is less likely. During these early moments, the baby may start to cry, and I've heard mothers ask, "What's wrong?" or "What did I do wrong?" The answer is probably nothing—you will discover that babies cry for many reasons. In the crib you will find a bottle of formula or water. Or you may try breast-feeding; but be aware that neither breast milk nor colostrum (the protein-rich first milk) appears until the second or third day in most first-time mothers. Most babies, however, will happily suck or nuzzle against you anyway.

This is a *first* for both of you. Babies don't come with little instruction labels and they haven't read all the books. Be patient for both of you. Soon enough you will be actively engaged with your baby. You will become sensitive to the unique melody of your infant. After birth, although you and your baby are physically separated, you are both psychically connected. There is still a strong but now *invisible* cord tying you to each other. The prenatal relationship is ongoing and now growing and changing. Your newborn may soon be breast-feeding, taking nourishment directly from your body; if you are bottle-feeding, your baby still remains dependent upon you even after the actual cord is severed.

Unless you are rooming-in, you will be brought your baby every four hours or so for feeding. If your baby was either small (under five pounds) or large (over nine pounds) at birth, you may be given the baby more frequently to be fed.

FEEDING YOUR NEWBORN

If you are not rooming-in, you can't really know when your baby is hungry. The nurses literally have their hands full and will not bring the baby to you when she cries unless it happens to be time for feeding. The usual schedule is for the babies to feed at ten, two, and six, around the clock. If you delivered early in the morning, you probably won't get to see your baby until ten in the morning unless you make a big fuss. (This is because of the many hospital routines that take precedence in the early part of each day.) Often it's the new father who "carries on" and is sent to the nursery to retrieve the baby.

If you are rooming-in, you can feed the baby according to the baby's needs. It is probably preferable to room-in if you want to establish breast-feeding, because the "let-down reflex" begins in response to your baby's cry. (If you don't room-in, you can definitely still breast-feed; there will just be a little delay in getting started.) Remember, you don't make breast milk for several days after delivery.

If you are not rooming-in, the nurse will automatically bring you the baby at two o'clock in the morning unless you specifically say you don't want the baby at that time. If you are feeling up—and there is often a "high" after birth—then take the baby. There are no distractions at 2 A.M., no calls or visitors. But if you want to skip this visit (maybe you are feeling as if you have been "to hell and back"), be sure to tell the nurse what you *do* want your baby to have—it could be water or formula. (It won't be breast milk, since it is virtually impossible for you to express enough or even any breast milk during this brief time in the hospital.)

NIGHTTIME

Be aware that there is a big difference between day- and nighttime at a hospital. In most hospitals your phone is turned off after nine o'clock in the evening, the lights are lower, and the staff is fewer.

Some women report a tremendous surge of energy, sometimes accompanied by fear and panic, in the middle of the night. Some psychologists say the new mother is feeling bereft —almost grieving for the baby that was part of her body for nine months. It's also possible that the panic is simply a result, if you are not rooming-in, of not knowing what is happening to your baby. If you find yourself pacing the floor, just pace right over to the nursery. If at *any* time, day or night, you miss your baby, take a walk and look at what my son likes to call the "glass house for babies." You may want to take the baby back to your room—just to hold her or sing to her. (When the fictional "Murphy Brown" was alone for the first time with her new son, she crooned her favorite, and appropriate, Aretha Franklin song, "You Make Me Feel Like a Natural Woman.")

VISITORS

Keep in mind, whether you are rooming-in or not, that the hospital usually limits visitors—both in number and in how long they can stay. You may think it's unfair that all the new grandparents can't come in and coo over the baby at once, but in fact you may be grateful for the restrictions. In general most hospitals have two brief visiting periods a day. If you have other children, encourage them to visit just as soon as they can. I also advise women to bring along a picture of their older children and tape it to the inside of the newborn's crib: this is one way your new baby can be introduced to her family; and more important, when the older siblings come to visit, they will feel automatically connected to the newest member of their family. The exception to the "no visitor" rule is Dad, who is usually allowed to practically room-in himself.

THE STAY: MOTHER CARE

As informed and ready for pregnancy and childbirth as a woman can be, no one can fully prepare you for this wonderful and yet frightening experience. Yes, it's a blessed event, but it is also often a painful and distressing experience. You are to-tally enveloped in what I call the "guts and glory" of new motherhood.

Labor exacts both a psychological and a physical price. For some the cost of delivering a baby is greater than for others.

Let me comfort you with the knowledge that much of what you are *feeling*, especially in the first twenty-four to forty-eight hours, is a result of the cacophony of hormones released when the baby is born. It's not all in your head; it's in your blood-stream. After childbirth, a variety of reproductive hormones are indeed raging, buffeting you from all directions. Estrogen, pro-gesterone, oxytocin, and pitocin are just some of the hormones whose balance has to be reestablished from pregnancy to post-pregnancy. (It's also been observed that the level of a neural hormone called serotonin, which is related directly to mood, drops off just after delivery, sometimes as much as it does in people who've experienced a recent loss.)

Labor often leaves you with a lot of *physical* ills: You may be hypertensive, hypoglycemic, and bloated. Some new mothers mistakenly believe that childbirth will immediately "cure" some of the ailments they suffered with during pregnancy. But, for example, it takes at least forty-eight hours after birth for nasal discomfort and congestion to disappear. (I've heard more than one mom ask, "How come my nose is still stuffed?") And it can take weeks for a pregnancy rash to fade.

Even worse, many women leave the delivery room with a new baby *and* a brand-new case of hemorrhoids. Even if you had a C-section, unless it was a totally planned C-section, there was still a lot of pushing and you may indeed get hemor-rhoids. About one third of all women wind up with hemor-rhoids after delivery, though some cases are more bothersome than others. The nurses will usually give you an inflatable doughnut to sit on when you go to the bathroom so you don't hurt as much when you push. Stool softeners are also helpful. In some cases your doctor may prescribe a cream to help shrink your hemorrhoids.

The first time you try to have a bowel movement may be quite painful. You are not sure you won't just break open and fall apart. You won't, but you may have some leakage of blood. And when you urinate, it might not be in a single stream the way it used to be—it may be more like a shower. This will change. (The nurses will encourage you to drink lots of liquid so that you urinate frequently.) You'll usually feel more com-fortable if you hold your hand or a pillow firmly against your abdomen while you are urinating or having a bowel movement. You may be offered a laxative, which can make the difference between a hard and difficult stool or a soft and easier one to pass. If it's still painful, tell your doctor.

It's important to start walking as soon as you can after delivery. But when you do stand up, you will probably notice that you still look pregnant. (After I delivered my first child, I became impatient in the recovery room, so I abused my "doctor's privileges" and walked up the staff staircase to the nursery. I literally bumped into a fellow doctor, who asked, "When are you due?"—which dealt a momentary blow to my vanity!) I recommend that you walk as much as you like to the nursery, but *not* over to the scale. (The baby, the placenta, and the amniotic fluid added all together weigh only about twelve pounds. You probably have at least another twenty to "explain away.") There will also be a lot of fluid shifting, so I suggest you wait at least a week before weighing in. To make yourself feel better during your stay, wash your hair, put on makeup, or do whatever it takes so you feel as lovely as everyone says the new baby is.

CESAREAN SECTIONS

C-sections present a different set of challenges to a new mom. In an elective or planned C-section, a small horizontal incision is made at the lower part of the abdomen around four inches in length. If you had what we call a "crash" or emergency C-section, then the scar runs up and down and may be quite long and raised. In either case, the trend is to help you sit up and walk the same or very next day. (In the past, "C-section women" stayed in the hospital up to two weeks and didn't get up out of bed until the fourth day.)

"C-section mothers" often feel pretty good the very

The typical C-section scar is small and follows the
"bikini line." The longer vertical scar in emergency
cesarean procedures will also heal well in time.

next day and then lousy two days later. If you
hadn't been pushing and going through the several
stages of labor for hours and hours, then you may
even feel "up" for the first day or so after the delivery. Usually you are able to walk to the bathroom,
although you may be afraid your stitches will "burst
open"—and it's easier to have a bowel movement if
you've had a C-section. The discomfort on the second day has to do with the natural healing process:
when the stitches are fresh and holding together
nicely, you tend to feel better than when the scar is
actually forming and the stitches start tugging and
contracting. (The skin heals by knitting together,
and that process hurts.) By the second day you may
need pain relief—there are a variety of pain medica-
tions which can be given to you, and you should request one when you are hurting.

You probably will not have breast milk or colostrum

until the third, fourth, or even fifth day. Why does it take longer for your milk to come in than it does after a vaginal delivery? When you are in pain, which is a form of stress, the body's response is to decrease the release of the hormone that is responsible for initiating the flow of milk. Even so, if you are not yet making milk and you are planning to breast-feed, you should be "practicing"—it's a good learning experience for the baby to suck and for you to find comfortable positions. You can also enlist the father's help in positioning the baby for breast-feeding by placing pillows under your arms or by practicing the "football position," in which the baby is not lying across your abdomen but along your side with legs out back and head raised to the breast. (See illustration on p. 81.)

The biggest difference between a C-section and a vaginal delivery is that *you* have had a major operation and you need to take special care of your own health. You may opt for a nurse to help you at home. Going back to your regular life—exercising, driving a car, even bathing—is postponed longer.

In addition to the physical scars, it sometimes leaves behind very painful psychological ones. Childbirth classes rarely discuss C-sections and usually just dismiss them with a sentence or two as if they rarely happen. Understand that C-sections account for up to one third of all deliveries in the United States. I've heard new mothers say, "I went through all that labor for *nothing*," losing sight that they didn't go through it for nothing but for that precious bundle which is now in their arms. Often women have the feeling that they have somehow failed if they had a C-section. In my new mothers' groups I hear that echoed over and over. One mom said, "My friend was pregnant at the same time I was, and she said, 'Well, I wouldn't *let* a C-section happen to me.' " (Obviously, a C-section is not something you "let happen" to you but is medically necessary.) However, mothers who've had a real struggle getting pregnant or going full term don't much care *how* they had the baby.

GOING HOME

On your last day in the hospital, you will be given a document by the nurse with vital information for you to keep and another paper for you to fill out. The first will list the baby's birth weight, length, and blood type. The second asks you to name the baby. Don't feel pressured into choosing a name. All you need to do is write Baby Girl Cohen or Baby Boy O'Brien. It's not essential to name the baby at that moment. (Later you can request a form from your state's registry to give your baby a proper name.)

A word about leaving: If you know your baby is jaundiced, you may have to leave the hospital without her. It's a very disappointed and sad mother who goes home without her beautiful birthday package. Remember that jaundice is *not* a disease and for the short time you are separated you can visit her as often as you like. If, however, *you* are not feeling completely well, you can talk to your obstetrician about staying an extra day. More often than not, the baby has to stay only one extra day—if it's more than that, you will be discharged before the baby is.

The night before you are expecting to be discharged, send any flowers, balloons, or gifts you have received home with your partner. Make sure you have clothes to go home in; do not have your partner bring you your regular-size jeans. You will do better to go home in something comfortable like a sweatpants outfit that would fit a six-months-pregnant woman.

LAYETTE FOR THE FIRST 6–8 WEEKS

CLOTHING

3 dozen cloth or disposable diapers (or 1 dozen cloth if using disposables to use as spit-up wipers)
2–3 pair diaper pins or clips (for cloth diapers)
3–6 pair cloth diaper cover-ups—Velcro type closures preferable
6–12 newborn undershirts
6–8 short-sleeved tops or long "kimonos" for warm weather
6–8 long drawstring nightgowns and/or newborn jumpsuits for cool weather and nights
2–4 warm buntings or sleep suits for daytime outings and nighttime sleeping in cold weather
1–2 sun hats (warm weather)
1–2 warm hats (cold weather)
2–3 pair washable booties or socks
1–2 very small sweaters, preferably cotton

BEDDING

6–12 receiving blankets
6–12 sets of rubber pads and soaker mats to change baby on and protect laps and sheets
3–6 crib sheets
2–3 baby towels, extra soft, absorbent, possibly with a hood
3–6 baby washcloths
2–4 medium-weight washable blankets

SUPPLIES

Mild soap for bathing the baby—with moisturizer
Mild soap for washing the baby's clothes
Fabric softener for the baby's diapers and clothes
Diaper bucket
Rectal thermometer
Vaseline and diaper rash ointment, preferably with zinc oxide
2–3 pacifiers
Small, somewhat stiff hairbrush
Formula (for bottle-fed babies)—small cans or powder
6–8 bottles for water, formula, or expressed breast milk

EQUIPMENT

Bassinet
Cradle, carriage, or crib for the baby to sleep in
Dresser or shelves to store the baby's clothes
Padded, *secure* changing table or surface

Small square plastic basin or baby bathtub
Infant chest carrier
Infant car safety seat
Portable bed or carry basket
Tote bag for diapers, extra clothes, etc.

When it's time to leave, you will need a receiving blanket
and an outfit for the baby that has been washed in advance.
There is a stiffness in some infant clothes which needs to be
prewashed. (Use a detergent that will not destroy the flame-
retardant properties in the baby clothes. It should say "flame-
retardant-safe" right on the box.) Find out what the hospital
discharge time is, and make sure you give yourself plenty of
time to dress the baby. The inner clothes, including the under-
shirt, should be 100 percent cotton. Make sure the outfit you
choose has legs rather than a "sac" style so that you can easily
get her into an infant car seat (the law in most states). Many
people learn the hard way, on their knees in the backseat trying
desperately to stuff a baby in a blanket sleeper into a car seat.
(In most climates you need a cotton hat for the baby.)

The morning you are going to leave, the pediatrician will
come in and either deliver a speech on baby care—covering
anything and everything from feeding to bathing and diapering
—or she might hand you some pamphlets. (At some point
during your stay there should be an opportunity to watch bathing and feeding demonstrations conducted by nurses.) Make
sure you have a pen and paper ready to write down any questions that come up. Before you leave, it's important to ask
what the baby's weight at discharge is. It will give you perspec-
tive when you see the pediatrician two weeks later.

All kinds of paperwork gets exchanged between the doctors
and the nurses. Then the moment will come when the nurse
walks in and asks, "Are you ready?" You may think, "Not
really." The nurses will check your armband and your baby's
armband one last time and hand you a copy of the birth certificate, which also lists the baby's birth weight and the certifi-

cate number you read off to the nurses each time they brought you the baby. (You will be handed a small folder, which you will use later, to record your baby's immunizations and doctor visits.) The hospital may give you some formula, if you've been using it, and sometimes a gift basket filled with baby care products.

You may even have to deal with the cashier's office before you can take the baby out. In some hospitals you must sit in a wheelchair with the baby on your lap until you exit the hospital door. More commonly you are escorted out on foot with the baby in your arms. It's an incredible private moment when you take possession of your baby. You come out of the hospital with a big, special present—your baby.

You are on your way home.

It's time to say goodbye to the hospital and hello to your new life.

PART II:
TENDER LOVING CARE: MOTHERS

CHAPTER 3

Homecoming: The New Family

$\mathcal{I}$f time seems to slow down in the delivery room, when you arrive home, time may seem upside down and inside out. New mothers may feel like Alice in the looking glass: they experience wonder and puzzlement as they see a reflection they are not yet familiar with. I tell mothers: You left the house as an expectant mother and you come home a mommy!

The door shuts. You are home. Looking back at this moment, most women recall having a lot to do. I clearly remember walking into my apartment with the baby in my arms and thinking: I have to check the answering machine for messages. Do the plants need watering? Is there enough milk in the refrigerator? Has the dog been walked today? I was concerned with all the details of our daily lives. I found myself behaving the way I *always* did when I walked in the door. In addition to everything else I worry about, having a new baby meant adding one more thing to my "to do" list. The world on my shoulders had just gotten heavier!

At my new mothers' groups, many moms confess that they spent the first hours or so home from the hospital not as "magically" as they had imagined. The fantasy of the fairy-tale-like entrance was replaced with visions of their responsibilities dancing in their heads. As one mom said, "I walked in the door and I heard myself shouting, 'Why are all the dishes still in the sink?' and 'Where's the bassinet?' " (Many prospective parents are superstitious and wait to have the nursery furniture delivered; it's not uncommon, in fact, for baby furniture companies to proclaim: "We deliver when *you* deliver.")

Friends and relatives may want to be there for your homecoming, but this is a special private moment in time that occurs only once with this baby. Many moms tell me that the last thing they wanted when they got home was a parade of people coming to admire the baby—but that's just what they got.

In the hospital, think about what kind of homecoming you want, and if you decide you want to be alone, then specifically ask friends and relatives not to be there. When I discussed this with an expectant couple recently, the mom-to-be nudged her husband and said, "I told you your mother doesn't *need* to be there." Yet there are those women who specifically want their *own* mother to be there for them. A brand-new mom may be very proud to share being a mother with her own "mommy."

My suggestion is that when you first come home, forget the chores and go into the room where your baby will be sleeping —possibly in your own bedroom. Unplug the phone. Close the door. I strongly recommend that you spend the next few hours in that environment. This little interlude in time is a gift for you, your baby, and your mate. Being alone with each other now is often more important in terms of bonding than was the actual moment of birth.

New mothers who take these hours for themselves are overwhelmingly glad they did. But don't be surprised if you are accused of being selfish, silly, or neurotic by all those friends and relatives to whom you said "I want to be alone"! If necessary, say it was your pediatrician's advice. I explain that it is, in fact, natural to do this: In many cultures the mother and baby are assigned to a midwife or assistant to help them with the transition from birth to after birth. They live separated from the community for up to six weeks with no male visitors. (This may have started out as part of some superstitious belief, but anthropologists, including the late Margaret Mead, have suggested that this custom may have evolved in order to ensure that new mothers get what they really needed: *time alone with the baby*, and away from responsibilities.)

After a few hours, when your baby has gradually become accustomed to the sight and sounds of her room, you can introduce her to the rest of the house. Take her for a grand tour and make her home a familiar place for her. Soon enough the television, radio, neighbors, and relatives will intrude and distract you.

Don't be surprised, however, if your faithful family pet isn't too eager to share his space with a new arrival. It's a good idea to get the pet used to the new baby even before you come home. For example, your partner could bring home a T-shirt that the baby has worn in the hospital. That will help your pet acquire a smell for the baby. When they meet for the first time, you don't want your pet to howl or hide.

I also recommend that at the end of the first twenty-four hours you touch base with your pediatrician. When I say goodbye on my final visit before discharge, I tell the new mother to keep a pad by her side and jot down any questions that come up after she leaves the hospital. I suggest she call me in twenty-four hours. She usually says, "Oh, I'll only call if I have questions." Enough questions generally accumulate after twenty-four hours to warrant a chat.

It's a good time, after these twenty-four hours, to sit back and take a big breath. When I ask the mother how *she* is doing, I invariably hear a great big sigh! What often happens in that first day home is that you have been searching for patterns to rely on, but there aren't any yet. Instead, you need to accept unpredictability. Your baby is very different today than she was just the day before. (I just smile when the mother of a one-week-old says, "But she *used* to sleep for three hours at a time," or "She *used* to have a bowel movement once a day.") It's too early for any predictable patterns to have developed yet. Your baby may at times be very wakeful or very sleepy, very hungry or suddenly fussy—all of which is perfectly normal for newborns. You will soon enough come to know your baby and how to make a space for her in your life.

I always give this advice: *Simplify your life.* Tell yourself in advance that you are not going to earn an A for every task. For starters, decide you are not going to bother with the laundry. (Try to make sure there's a week's supply of clean clothes before you leave for the hospital.) Remember all those friends and relatives who asked if there was anything they could do for you? Tell them *yes.* Make a list *before* you even go to the hospital. Maybe a friend could straighten up the apartment before you get there. It may be a mess, and you don't want to have to coordinate details from the hospital. Does someone need to assemble whatever furniture may have been delivered? Have someone greet the baby nurse (if you are having one). You probably don't want to meet her at the hospital.

LETTING IN THE REST OF THE WORLD

Soon enough there will come the time when you will throw open your doors and welcome the friends, neighbors, and relatives who come to celebrate the newest member of your family.

There is tremendous pleasure and pride in showing off your baby to others. It's hard for adults to pass up caressing a newborn. Recently there seems to be a return to the old belief that newborns shouldn't be picked up or touched by anyone but the parents. I don't subscribe to that. Obviously if a friend has a cold, she shouldn't pick up the baby, and toddlers in particular should have limited access to the newborn. That's simply because toddlers are famous for breaking out in chicken pox or strep throat or the very common cold just hours after they've visited you. (And their hygiene leaves a lot to be desired.) But no matter what, if it's *your* toddler who wants to pick up her new baby brother, then go for it (with supervision, of course). It's part of the package of being a family.

Well-meaning relatives will want to share with you *all* their own experiences, which may or may not be helpful. My advice is to listen with one ear, smile, and take everything with a grain of salt. You need to experience your baby for yourself. Child-rearing notions change—and people have distorted memories. People often remember parenting the way they *wish* it had been and not necessarily the way it actually was. (My mother-in-law often recalled that her son slept through the night when he was only one week old and spoke at six months! I recently overheard a mother of a teenager saying, "Oh, when my son was a baby, he never cried. He just looked at me and I knew exactly what he wanted.") My advice is to trust your own instincts.

Let's get one thing straight. *This is your baby.* So don't be intimidated by your mother, your mother-in-law, your best friend, or your baby nurse.

My First Golden Rule for Parents is: *Babies are not fragile.* I must get thousands of questions which stem from the underlying sense that babies are fragile and can splinter like glass. Although they appear to be soft and vulnerable creatures, they are really pretty tough. Even the so-called soft spot is covered by a thick membrane.

My Second Rule is: *Babies are not sterile*—so they don't need to be handled with surgical gloves. You will save a lot of precious time, for instance, if you don't rewash everything of baby's that touches the carpet.

NEW ROLES

You not only became a mother when you were handed your newborn, but automatically became part of a new extended family. There can be a wonderful sense of symmetry to the continuing life cycle. When one of my new mothers broke her arm, she called her own father to help her with the baby, because her husband was out of town. Her father's response was to rush right over. As this mom put it, "It occurred to me that once you become a parent, you are a parent forever. Even though I now have a baby of my own, I will always be my daddy's child. That was really nice to know."

Family
You will undoubtedly have a different relationship with your own parents. Grandparents often claim "ownership" of the new baby and can step over imaginary boundaries as they stake out their territorial rights. (As one woman explained, "It's not surprising that my parents want to be around a lot. My son has my father's name.") New mothers occasionally find they now have a somewhat tense relationship with their own mothers. I hear new mothers complaining they feel "infantilized"— treated as if they are suddenly not competent or capable of taking care of a baby. The torrent of advice can be unwanted and even insulting. ("You must be doing something wrong. You never cried when you were a baby.")

Don't be too quick to give thumbs down to all their advice. Maybe your mother has a different way of holding your daughter that really seems to soothe her. Try not to pounce every time your mother intervenes. Let's say your son has hiccups, which doesn't concern you in the least, but your mother jumps up, dips her finger in sugar, and then puts it in your son's mouth. You may be horrified at the scene, but your mother is just repeating what *her* mother taught her. Both you and your baby can "swallow" (or at least tolerate) most of your parents' advice. (By the way, the sugar doesn't work.)

On the positive side, try to see grandparents as the people who will love, cherish, (and baby-sit) your baby.

Don't be surprised if you are suddenly elevated in status with your in-laws. As one mother explained, "I had a very neutral relationship with my in-laws until I gave them their little 'prince.' Then it all changed. They are much nicer as grandparents than they were as in-laws." They are also around more often. Unfortunately, the extra attention—the daily phone calls and surprise visits—is not always welcome. Hopefully you'll all learn to strike an acceptable balance.

Friends

Your relationship with friends who don't have children will not be the same; you are now on different sides of the looking glass! Initially friends will come to visit bearing balloons and gifts. One mother sadly reported that a good friend came over to meet the baby and never came back again. She also reluctantly admitted that, yes, the baby was the focus of the entire evening. Most women without children are not fascinated with the details of baby care. (As another friend said to a new mother, "Do you realize how boring you've become?" "Boring" probably wasn't the right word; "obsessed" with her new daughter was more accurate.)

Old friends are not quite sure how to treat you. They ask you to go out, as usual, to the movies on Saturday night and you think, "I'd rather be home with my baby." If they invite you over for dinner, they may be concerned that you will bring the baby. And you may be offended if they *don't* include the baby. At the same time, they may not realize how hard it is for you to get a sitter—and that you might not want to get one just yet.

It's almost as if you speak different languages. A single friend, Beth, complained to me about her friend Nora, who had become a mother. Nora went to the theater, and when she called home, the sitter said the baby wouldn't stop crying. Nora immediately called up her friend Beth and asked her to go over and check that the baby was really all right. Beth went reluctantly, but she was annoyed almost beyond words at her "paranoid" and inconsiderate friend. She didn't understand at all until a few years later when *she* had her first child.

There's no question that you will have to reach out and make your old friends comfortable. Preserve those relationships that are worth saving. The first few months are critical as to whether a particular friendship will even continue.

You may find yourself drawn closer to the friends who already have children. They'll love you for asking advice and will welcome you into the informal mommy club.

Becoming a new mother is a great opportunity to make lots of new friends. Don't be afraid to look a woman with a baby directly in the eye and start a conversation. When you were pregnant, strangers often broke the social ice with, "When are you due?" Now you can simply ask, "How old is the baby?" Long days can be made to seem much shorter when they are shared with another mother and baby. You may almost feel as if you were back in kindergarten: you meet "neat" kids (of all ages); you get to play with toys; you get to go to the park and the zoo.

The New Father

In the hospital elevator recently, I watched as a couple went home with their newborn. The father was lovingly cradling the baby when the mother reached for her. The dad said, "You carried her for nine months; let me have a turn." Dads are parents too, but too often we neglect the new dad and all of his feelings.

It would be a great loss to your baby and to the father for him to be left out. Babies benefit from the love and care of both parents. Tender loving care can be dispensed by dads—most of whom are willing to participate even if they look to Mom for guidance. Unfortunately, dads are often relegated to the role of observer.

You don't bond by having philosophical discussions. You bond by taking care of your baby—by changing his diaper and having him smile when you nuzzle his stomach. If you say, "My husband doesn't like to do those sorts of things, so I do them," you are cheating everyone. A father, however, is not a male mother. Fathers father differently from the way mothers mother. Although there are a lot of functions you can both do, the style with which you do them is different. Your baby will

The marital spotlight shifts from the couple and
shines on the baby; it's usually the mother who
controls the beam.

benefit from the differences. (So, when Dad is with the baby,
don't peek over his shoulder to see if he's doing it "right." He's
nervous too and may think you were somehow born with a
diapering or bathing gene!)

It is difficult for your husband to be left out of a relationship that is clearly pleasurable to you. Force yourself to let
go and let him derive the same pleasures you get from bathing the baby, even diapering and all that kissing and snug-
gling. (A mother who realized her son needed her husband's
attention as well marveled, "I can see him falling in love
with my husband.") Some women get angry with the father
for not participating in the "hard" part but sometimes they
don't let him in to do the "easy" and wonderful part—the
loving. Your husband can't grow to be attached to the baby
unless he has a lot of physical contact. Help him be part of
the new trio. You can *all* lie on the bed together and cuddle.

It really is delicious to have all the people you love the most right beside you. Savor these precious moments.

Remember that your husband returned from the hospital in a new role just as you did—he just didn't have the same dramatic bodily changes, although he may have gained a few pounds eating along with you. (I recently conducted a little survey and discovered the average weight gain for fathers was about six pounds!) In my office, one expectant father asked a new father, "How does life change after the baby?" The new father replied, "Life doesn't change. You just start a whole new one."

During the evolution of this new life, the creation of the relationship with the baby is all-consuming. The marital spotlight shifts from the couple and shines on the baby, and it's usually the wife who controls the beam. The husband experiences this period differently—but he has valid experiences of his own.

CHAPTER 4

The Fourth Trimester

Some pregnant women imagine that after giving birth their bodies will quickly turn back nine months, like the resetting of a clock, but of course, it's not like that at all. The truth is that you've replaced one set of discomforts with another. When you were pregnant, you went to the bathroom practically all the time; now you don't go nearly as often but your bladder control is poor. You spent sleepless nights trying to find a comfortable position; now you can find the position, but you *still* have sleepless nights because the baby keeps waking up.

I remember after my first child was born I almost wished the baby were back inside me. It was easier to be pregnant than to be the mother of a newborn. This is generally referred to as the postpartum period. I prefer to call it the "fourth trimester."

How well you survive the fourth trimester has a lot to do with your *expectations* for both your physical and psychological well-being. Try not to pay too much attention to the story about your neighbor who bounced back from pregnancy and returned to work in three days or to your hospital roommate, who zipped up her size 6 jeans and waltzed out of bed. There really is a wide range of normal recovery patterns, and you probably will fall somewhere in the middle. It's been my experience that the vast majority of new mothers are not zipping up their jeans and dashing off to work—but those exceptions are the ones that grab our attention.

TENDER LOVING CARE: YOUR PSYCHOLOGICAL NEEDS

On the psychological front, much of what you are feeling is still under hormonal regulation. As a result of your hormone swings, you may be prone to strong emotions. For reasons which are not entirely clear, these are usually *negative* emotions. The feelings we typically associate with the postpartum period are insecurity (for example, you might wake up in the middle of the night and decide that everything you have bought for the baby is somehow wrong), sadness (including crying jags), anger, and irrational fears—such as deciding that your next-door neighbor is really Jack the Ripper incarnate. It's as if your body is in a constant state of vigilance. These feelings are hormonally programmed reactions probably designed in order to protect the species. The changes in hormones are similar to the changes that occur in what's known as the fight-or-flight phenomenon: your body is ready to "retreat" or "attack," depending on the situation. This is the state the new mother often finds herself in. She is anxious and ready to leap.

No matter what other feelings you are experiencing, you will automatically *protect* this new baby of yours—in ways you can not even imagine. A new mother recently came out of the hospital with her infant in her arms and tripped on the stairs (a very uncommon occurrence). Normally it is reflexive to put your arms out to break your fall. But this woman stopped herself with her face and was rewarded with a broken nose. Only her pediatrician totally understood that this woman, now a mother, could not, would not, put her arms out and let her baby fall! (Mother and baby are now doing just fine.)

You may mistakenly label your mood during this period as "postpartum depression" when in fact postpartum depression is a specific, serious illness. (See Box, p. 60) What you most

Try to rest when your baby is sleeping, making sure
you are lying in a secure position.

likely have is a case of the "baby blues," which is a state of
mind, not an illness. You can console yourself that much of
what you *do* while experiencing the blues is reversible, and
almost anything you *say* will be forgiven, if not instantly for-
gotten. New mothers often display the symptoms of the baby
blues to anyone who is around. So one mother may say, "I
wish I never had this baby." Another will accuse her own
mother: "You don't know anything about raising a baby"—as if
she hadn't even raised her. Yet another mom will turn to her
husband and complain, "You don't understand, and you're
never here when I need you."

These outbursts can come on uncontrollably—a bit like being possessed by a "harpy"—but rarely do they have any lasting
impact on the development of your family. Let me assure
you, this brief period will pass. Most husbands are forgiving. I
like to joke, "If you find yourself bewitched and bothered,

Don't expect to slip right into your pre-pregnancy
clothing. Understand that your body needs time to
return to what it was.

your husband is probably more than a little 'bewildered' himself."

No matter how lousy you may feel, it's particularly important that you don't isolate yourself from others. If you can, this
is the perfect time to join a new mothers' group. (Call your
pediatrician, obstetrician, or childbirth educator for leads and
check bulletin boards in doctors' offices as well.) When I run
groups, mothers often say, "I wish I had been here the first
week after I got home." What's crucial is the acknowledgment
that what one mother is feeling is being shared by almost all
the mothers. Sharing feelings is a wonderful antidote to the
blues. It's important to realize that you can be thrilled and
delighted with your newborn *and* also exhausted and resentful
at the same time. One feeling doesn't negate the other. Motherhood is never an either/or proposition.

It was at one of my new mothers' groups that a mother first

Twins can be twice the pleasure, but expect more
than twice the work at times. Be creative and don't
hesitate to ask for help when you need it.

confessed that she felt like an "invisible woman." As she said
that, mothers around the room started to nod their heads in
agreement. A strange but not scientifically proven phenomenon often happens as soon as the baby is born: Moms slowly
fade. Even in the hospital, everyone rushes over to the nursery.
As one mom said, "I remember thinking, what about *me?* I'm
part of the birth day too." (I recently visited a new mother and
baby in the hospital, and the mother asked her husband to
bring her a hair dryer so she could "do" her hair. Her husband
responded, "Why? No one will be looking at *you.*") Now that a
few weeks have passed, that same mother lamented: "I'm
thinking of going on vacation since I feel superfluous. Nobody
ever asks me how *I* am."

You will have to find your own ways to color yourself back
into life. Be good to yourself every opportunity you get. If
you ever learned transcendental meditation in college, this is

Use any free time to spend a few quiet, peaceful
moments. Meditation and yoga are just two of
many ways to relax.

a good time to start chanting again. Or do yoga breathing
(*not* delivery breathing). Play music you really like. Rent
happy movies. And make sure you smile whenever you pass
another mother—empathy really works wonders in the healing process.

POSTPARTUM DEPRESSION

PPD is a real illness with its own symptoms. It is a
very significant though little-written-about condition.
It differs from "baby blues" both in severity and in
symptoms, though some overlap exists and can lead
to a delay in diagnosis. For a long time PPD was dis-
missed as not being a "real" condition and women

Periods of detachment or sadness are not
uncommon in the first weeks after delivery,
particularly at those moments when it is difficult
to satisfy your baby. These short but intense
episodes are known as "baby blues."

who found themselves with symptoms were considered to have underlying psychiatric instability that the
stress of motherhood happened to uncover. No wonder so few women ever sought help until recently.

PPD is estimated to occur in 2 per 3,000 deliveries,
which translates to about 370,000 women in the
United States each year. PPD is the hormonally and
biochemically induced reaction to the body's up-
heaval in giving birth. Its symptoms coincide with the
sudden and dramatic drop in progesterone and estrogen levels and the similar reduction in neural hormones and endorphins. Even the thyroid and adrenal
hormones (cortisone) which have been pumping
throughout pregnancy take a dive. All this drama
begins within twenty-four to thirty-six hours of
delivery.

A wise mother sleeps when her baby sleeps. It's also
a wonderful opportunity to feel close to your
newborn.

The symptoms of PPD may include anxiety, paranoia, detached feelings (particularly concerning the
baby), sleeplessness, loss of appetite, loss of sexual desire, uncontrollable crying, hallucinations, and even
suicidal behavior. In its severest form, it usually leads
to hospitalization.

On the other hand, "baby blues" usually have some
relationship to the circumstances around the birth
(difficult delivery, a C-section when you were determined not to have one, too many responsibilities),
and often is limited to mildly depressive symptoms
and tearfulness. A woman may experience self-doubt
and a lack of enthusiasm over her new role but nothing like the passionate depths of despair associated
with PPD.

Usually all the major symptoms have resolved by

the fourth month, but the memories of this time may last a lifetime.

TENDER LOVING CARE: YOUR PHYSICAL NEEDS

Don't neglect yourself. Get some sleep. Take the opportunity whenever your baby is asleep to do the same—the thank-you notes will wait. Even if you feel as though you have no time for yourself, find the time. Looking good makes you feel better when those uninvited friends show up. (And they will show up, protesting, "I know you didn't mean *me* when you said no visitors.")

As I've said, your body does not miraculously return to its prenatal state, though you might assume it *should*. Now there's even a "pregnant doll" on the market—after the baby "pops out," the stomach immediately becomes flat as a board!

HYGIENE AND AFTERCARE

Personal cleanliness was probably something you always took for granted. Of course you want to be clean and well groomed, but now you have to renegotiate on your body's terms.

In the first weeks, showering is preferable to bathing, and you really shouldn't bathe until the doctor tells you it's all right. You may need your partner to help you get in and out of the shower. Don't be surprised if you leak breast milk in the shower.

You have to pay particular attention to your vaginal area. For general hygiene there are pads saturated with witch hazel known as Tucks which both cleanse and soothe. Every time you go to the bathroom, squirt warm water on your vaginal area. You may have been given a little plastic squirt bottle in the hospital: I continued to use that bottle for weeks after I got home. After I squirted the water, I would see little clots of blood in the toilet bowl, which is perfectly normal. All new mothers, even C-section mothers, experience some vaginal bleeding. Vaginal bleeding is hormonal bleeding—the shedding of the lining of the uterus. (Advice: You never know when you will bleed, or how much bleeding there will be, so wear a sanitary napkin and avoid wearing white clothes for the first few weeks.)

Your bladder control may be poor, and you may leak a little urine. Practice stopping yourself from urinating by tightening your muscles (Kegel exercises). Empty your bladder often. (As your uterus shrinks, it relieves the pressure on the bladder, which leads to a natural return of function.)

You have to pay particular attention to all your body parts that were affected by the birth.

- If you had a *C-section*, your stitches were removed in the hospital, but the incision site still needs some attention. The best way to clean your scar or healing wound is to use a soapy washcloth. Wet the washcloth and squeeze it over your abdomen so that the soapy water runs down over the stitches. Don't directly rub the scar or it could hurt or disrupt the scab which is forming. (Use the washcloth and rinse again with clear water or just let the shower water run over you.)
- If you had an *episiotomy*, treat it similarly as you would the incision in a C-section. Squeeze the washcloth over the area and use a spray bottle. Once you are permitted to take a bath, the general rule is: The more swelling, the more you should use cold; the less swelling, the more warmth feels good. (You may also discover that sitting on hard surfaces feels better than soft.)
- Your *breasts* need special attention whether or not you are breast-feeding. If you *are* breast-feeding, the nipples may be tender and the breasts engorged. As your baby sucks, the nipple gets leathery and more accustomed to the action. The rest of the breast may be rock-hard and you may

Sometimes the pain and letdown after delivery can overshadow the experience.

see big blue veins around the center of the chest. (That's just evidence of the increased blood supply that your breasts require for production of milk.) The painful engorgement can be relieved with cool packs—just fill some Ziploc-type bags with ice cubes. (See page 78, "Breast-feeding," for special care of breasts.) If you are breast-feeding, you may also feel hot—it is quite normal to have a body temperature of 99–100°F. (If your temperature goes over 100.6°F, if your breasts feel tender, or there are warm red areas on either breast, then call the doctor. It's probably a blocked milk duct which may need more attention and/or medication.)

Even if you are *not* breast-feeding, you may have some discomfort. Don't be surprised if your breasts are a bit swollen even a week after birth. Although you are bottle-feeding, it takes your body a while to figure that out and to stop producing the hormones that would turn on milk production. Since there is no demand for milk, there will be no supply. Your breasts will shrink back but you may still have stretch marks.

- Unfortunately, your *hemorrhoids* may have traveled home with you from the hospital. Until you can take a real bath, try sitting in a baby bathtub filled with water on the floor of the bathroom. Use something sturdy as a brace to lower yourself. (Invariably, just as you get into the tub, maybe with a book on your knees, the phone rings! Turn the ringer off before you attempt a bath.) It's important that you keep your stools soft. (If the doctor encouraged you to continue to take your prenatal vitamins, your stools may be hard because the vitamins are high in iron.) Take stool softeners and drink lots and lots of fluid to help keep your stools from hardening. Remember that the harder you push, the bigger and more swollen and tender those hemorrhoids become. Apply either an over-the-counter hydrocortisone cream or hemorrhoid preparation. (If necessary, your doctor will prescribe a stronger cream to help shrink them.)

TAKING INVENTORY: FROM HEAD TO TOE

If you stand naked in front of a full-length mirror, you can see the inevitable and predictable changes in your body. (You may be reluctant to stand in front of the mirror due to these very same changes!)

- Start with your hair—you may experience sudden loss. Try not to use harsh products and use a detangler or conditioner so your hair won't pull out or break as easily.
- You may find you have brown spots on your face. Be careful not to expose your skin to the sun. Your skin will soon return to normal, but it will be drier during this period, and you may need extra moisturizer. (Some women de-

velop skin moles or get rashes during or right after pregnancy; usually these resolve spontaneously within a few
weeks or months.)

- You may appear to have a cold or just a stuffed nose; this
may be due to postpartum sinus swelling. Ask your doctor
about using a decongestant. Sauna and steam are also
good for sinus problems. While you were pregnant, you
were probably told to avoid hot rooms because they could
raise your blood pressure. Now it's good for you and your
skin, but to be safe, have your blood pressure checked.

- While you were pregnant, your entire skeletal alignment
changed: in order to carry the weight of the baby in front,
your pelvic bones had to spread apart and tilt slightly.
The distribution of weight on your knees and ankles was
very different too. You're still not walking or even standing the way you used to. In nine months you figured out
how to "waddle" so that your weight was over both fe-
murs (thighbones). All of a sudden the weight is gone—
lying over there in the bassinet. Your skeleton will gradually shift back and your old posture will return.

- Your feet may have grown and you may have gone up half
a shoe size. Although they usually shrink after giving
birth, they don't *always*, so don't buy shoes for at least
three months.

NUTRITION

New mothers still have specific nutritional needs. That's why
most obstetricians recommend you continue to take your prenatal vitamins for the first three months after pregnancy—particularly if you are nursing, but even if you are not. You have
just lost a large portion of your calcium, iron, and basic miner-
als to the baby. You need to replenish your supply.

You've lost a lot of fluid since the birth, but probably not a
lot of weight. So, again, don't head for the scale. If you are
typical, you lost about twelve to fifteen pounds in the hospital.

Forget about dieting, for at least a few weeks, and eat a well-balanced diet. If you have too rapid a weight loss (which is unlikely), you will be more prone to keep the stretch marks on your breasts even if you lose the pounds.

If you are a nursing mother, you will need a lot of fluids. Make sure there's *always* a pitcher of something you like waiting for you in the refrigerator. Try to drink the "right" kinds of fluids, such as water and decaffeinated herbal teas, and avoid sugary fruit juices or high-sodium vegetable juices and salty boullion, as these liquids will cause you to retain fluid. Feeling bloated is just as awful as feeling dehydrated. If you have waited nine long months to have a "real" cup of coffee, go for it, but in moderation. It may even have a diuretic effect on you. The same advice holds true for alcohol. I've had new mothers say, "I've been so good, can't I just have a glass of wine?" It's a tough call. I tell my new mothers: Never get intoxicated, but an occasional glass of wine with dinner will do no harm to the baby, and may do you some good.

PHYSICAL ACTIVITIES

In many ways you are limited in what you can do physically by your doctor, who probably advised you "don't do anything"—until your next visit. With the exception of heavy lifting and jumping, there are other physical activities you can enjoy. Just make sure to stop and listen to your body. You can certainly take walks—just put the baby in a Snugli and march out the door.

You need to strengthen your abdominal muscles. Every time you do something that requires lifting, such as picking up the baby, tuck your stomach in—this protects and strengthens your back muscles as well. Do tummy tucks, and keep doing the Kegel exercises you practiced during pregnancy.

Set aside some time for an exercise session—do some stretching and relaxation exercises. If you had a vaginal delivery and were in good physical shape before you became preg-

Exercise helps you return to your pre-pregnancy
state. Check with your doctor before beginning any
exercise program.

nant, slowly add some sit-ups. (There are exercise tapes specifically designed for postpregnancy which you can rent and try
out.) As the days go by, take longer and longer walks. If you
have access to a pool, you can get right back into the swim of
physical activity once you okay this with your obstetrician.

Caution: This is not the time to start or go back to high- or
even low-impact aerobic workouts. If you do, you may bleed
heavily. In fact, women who go right back to work without
giving themselves a few weeks off often have chronic bleeding
which can last up to a year and lead to anemia and chronic
malnutrition. If you are breast-feeding, it is advisable to wait at
least two hours after an aerobic workout before nursing to allow lactic acid to leave your body.

If doing an activity—such as climbing stairs—hurts, then try
to avoid the activity. (The motto here should be "No pain
equals gain.") In general, you will be told not to drive for the

first few weeks. The exception is if driving is the *only* way for you to go out and shop and no one else can be delegated to do this for you. Your blood loss can ebb and literally flow, so keep a towel on the seat of the car. You could suddenly get woozy while driving. Pull off the road immediately if you are not feeling well. In addition, the sitting position which is necessary for driving may be the cause of some pain.

WHEN TO CALL YOUR DOCTOR

You will be seeing your obstetrician in two weeks if you had a C-section, or in four weeks after a vaginal delivery. Contact your doctor right away if you experience any of the following:

- Excessive bleeding (saturating a sanitary napkin every hour for more than four hours)
- Bleeding with a foul-smelling odor
- Temperature of 101°F or above
- Shaking chills
- Constant lower abdominal pain
- A vein or area in your leg that feels sore and tender, or one leg swells more than the other
- A red, warm area on a sore breast
- Anxiety, depression, or sleeplessness that is escalating

MOM, AT SIX WEEKS

Although most mothers of six-week-olds are still subject to the "blues," the physical toll has usually lessened. If you are breast-feeding, your breasts aren't as engorged; stitches have healed; your episiotomy is tender but you are not afraid to have a bowel movement without a laxative. You can usually get

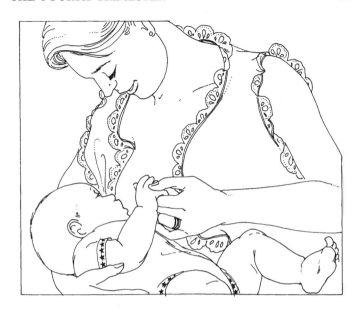

Feeding your baby should be a total experience
involving smell, touch, and sight as well as good
nutrition.

in and out of the bathtub without assistance. (You've been to
your doctor by now.)

The blues may still be "playing" because of fluctuating hormonal levels. You may, in fact, not experience a truly great day
until the estrogen level begins to rise back again. So don't be
surprised if you still cry occasionally. As one new mom said,
"Now that the baby is a few weeks old, I feel that I have *time*
to cry." Be nice to yourself right now, until your old self
catches up once again.

PART III:
TENDER LOVING CARE: BABIES

Introduction

$\mathcal{N}$ow it's time for the daily nitty-gritty of baby care. You may have experienced an initial euphoria after having the baby—as if you were sprinkled with "pixie dust"—but soon it blows away and reality sets in. A new mother's work is never "done" —mothering is full-time, around the clock—with the rewards measured in smiles and coos!

There has been a lot of discussion of so-called quality time, but you can't have quality *without* quantity. It's important that you don't underestimate the importance of what you are doing. Tender loving care is just that. When you feed your baby, for example, you are also helping him to develop trust. When you give him a bath, you do more than clean him—you are loving him as well.

Just as you are learning to mother, your husband should be learning to father. (I jokingly tell new parents: "Your baby needs a 'mother' bath *and* a 'father' bath.") Fortunately, more and more dads are actively participating in the daily care of babies. I now run new fathers' groups, though there is still more of a demand from new mothers. (At a new shopping center, I smiled at the sign on the men's bathroom which read: FATHERS' CHANGING STATION.) Of course, there are still those fathers who don't appreciate babies. As one dad told me, "I'll get more involved as soon as my son is a person." I told that father, "Your baby is not about to be a person. He's already a person, and you should get to know him."

As the days and weeks go by, you will no longer need the figurative equivalent of a crystal ball to predict your day; you'll have true hands-on experience at mothering, and will know what to expect. You may know, for example, that by ten in the morning, the baby will have been fed, bathed, and dressed and is ready for an outing. You'll also know that, despite all your best efforts, there will be those mornings when you're ready to go out but the baby's hungry, you feed him, he spits up, he needs a change of clothes, *you* need a change of clothes, he naps, and it's time to feed him once again. Eventually, however, you will start to develop routines you can generally rely on. (You'll know, for example, that the diapering, feeding, rediapering routine seems to take you anywhere from one to two hours.)

As the following chapters give you the basic facts you need to transform you from an amateur into an expert, don't be surprised if a friend who just had a baby now turns to *you* for advice!

CHAPTER *5*

● ●

Feeding

*F*eeding time provides a wonderful opportunity to be close to your newborn. You get your baby's undivided attention: when the baby is in your arms and you are feeding her, you are the closest you can be to her optimal visual distance. You hold her close and feed her; she looks into your eyes and she feels good. Babies associate the "yummy" sensations in their mouth with the warmth and love in your face. Feeding is the first step toward developing a trusting relationship with your baby.

EVERYBODY LOVES TO FEED BABIES

Even before giving birth, mothers usually have made the decision about whether or not they want to breast-feed. It may be a gut decision: you either *do* or *don't* want to breast-feed. Mothers rarely feel as strongly about whether to bottle-feed. The loaded emotional issues are tied to the decision to breast-feed.

Let me make my position clear: Although there are advantages connected to breast-feeding, it is *not* the only way to adequately nourish your child. We now have the capability of feeding babies healthfully with formula.

I am in favor of breast-feeding for the woman who wants to. Sometimes a drug that a mother is taking or an illness that a mother has may preclude her from breast-feeding. Anatomy *rarely* plays a part, but even then I've seen the most amazing things happen when a woman is determined to breast-feed. (For example, women with inverted nipples are often advised not to breast-feed—or to use a special "shield" which can help create enough suction to get the breast milk flowing. I've seen women with inverted or flat nipples who, after a few days of suction pumping, found that their nipples "popped" out.)

BREAST-FEEDING

Advantages

Breast milk is ideally suited for a baby's growth and development. (One of my mothers dubbed it the best "power breakfast.") It's nature's perfect product.

The well-known advantage to breast-feeding is that breast milk has immunological properties which no other substance has. No one has been able to exactly duplicate these properties in bottled milk. (Mothers often tell children, "Drink your milk, it's good for you." Nowhere is that more true than with breast milk.) New research shows that not only does nursing provide temporary protection against infection, but because maternal immune factors are transferred through milk, there is evidence that it also helps to trigger the baby's own immune system. (A protein component of breast milk activates certain white blood cells in the infant's body, causing them to develop sooner.) Another study found that breast-feeding has a preventive effect on urinary tract infections in both mother and infant.

Breast milk has a stimulating effect on a baby's bowel. It is also a natural stool softener, making it easier for the baby to pass meconium—the first stools. Breast-fed babies' stools are therefore generally soft and pass easily, often with every feed. Even if a mother breast-feeds for only a short time, it's still very helpful to the developing digestive system.

Breast-feeding is also practical: the milk is available, it's free,

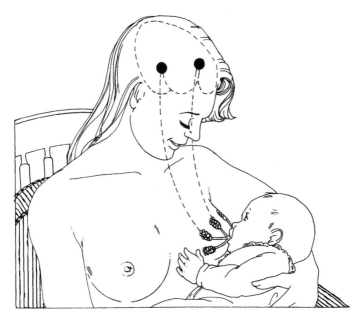

Your body is hormonally programmed to respond to
your baby's hunger by providing nourishment.

it's always at the right temperature, and it's there when you
need it.

Disadvantages

Breast-fed babies need to be fed more often than bottle-fed
babies. Many breast-feeding mothers must nurse about every
two hours—or twelve times a day for the first few weeks.
That's a lot of time spent feeding. Bottle-fed babies usually
require about six feedings per day, or every four hours. And not
all babies have the same feeding style: some feed like bar-
racudas and others are little gourmets. There are babies who
can empty your breast in five minutes, while others take
twenty minutes on just one side. There is no question it can be
exhausting, but all this feeding also has a purpose. Breast-feeding keeps you attached to your baby—both literally and figuratively—at a time when you can barely contemplate doing

much of anything else. The mechanics of breast-feeding require a great deal of commitment in time and attention. And
although the father can help, he cannot share feeding with you
(unless you express your milk and Dad uses a bottle—see section on fathers p. 99).

For at least the first month of your baby's life, you are frequently unable to leave the house for more than two hours at a
time, unless you plan to breast-feed outside. (Not all women
are comfortable breast-feeding outside the privacy of their
home. However, there are some cleverly designed clothes with
strategically placed flaps, so that you can breast-feed unnoticed
practically anywhere.) There are additional concerns if you
plan to go back to work and continue to nurse. How can you
express breast milk on the job without its interfering with
work? With a little ingenuity. (See "Back to Work," p. 183, for
advice on meeting the challenge of breast-feeding.) A television news producer told me that she was concerned about the
whirring sound her breast pump made at work, but her col-
leagues simply assumed she had a new high-power rewind button on her recording equipment!

It can be a disadvantage that everything *you* take into your
body passes to some extent into the breast milk. Breast-feeding
does force you to eat healthier, which is good, because the
elements in the food you eat pass to the baby. You and your
baby will have to come to peace with this. Some foods, such as
chocolate, which has some caffeine in it, may be harder to give
up than others. Only if you detect a connection between what
you've eaten and what your baby feels should you contemplate
a dietary restriction. And if you have a cocktail, your infant is
imbibing as well. Obviously when you take any medicine, so
does your baby. You will have to ask your doctor to clear each
and every drug you take—both prescribed and over-the-
counter. Also, breast-fed babies may require more of some specific vitamins such as A and D, since many mothers are themselves deficient in those vitamins and they don't pass well into

When bottle-feeding, hold your baby in a semi-upright position to help keep air from being swallowed and to reduce the chances of ear infection.

Find the positions that are most comfortable for you both—lying on your side is often restful and comfortable.

Lying with your baby head to tail can be a comfortable breast-feeding position.

breast milk. Most pediatricians routinely give breast-feeding mothers vitamins.

EARLY FEEDING

Most new mothers do not produce enough milk to express for at least a week, and conveniently newborns aren't born hungry. Mother Nature has the breast-feeding system all under control.

The earliest milk is called colostrum and it is produced in the last three weeks of pregnancy. First-time mothers usually don't produce even noticeable amounts of colostrum until the third day. Colostrum is richer in proteins and fat than regular breast milk, and is higher in immunoglobulins, which provide protection against a variety of illness. It also contains a protein, lactoferrin, which helps in the absorption of iron, and this helps prevent anemia. Colostrum is a clear to yellowish fluid, and sometimes mothers think they are not making any milk when they see this fluid. Remember that regular milk does not come in until about the third or fourth day.

Generally newborn babies eat next to nothing for a few days and are just fine, even though they are busy losing weight— about 5 percent of their birth weight in just the first week. However, this doesn't mean you shouldn't try to feed your baby. Just don't be surprised or upset if she sucks briefly and no milk appears. Putting your baby to your breast often helps prime the hormonal pump. And you both will be rewarded. Your baby will have the opportunity to learn to suck, and you are gaining by feeling close to your baby while your body is being stimulated to produce milk. It is important, however, that you don't let her suck forever. Sucking on a "dry" breast may be pleasurable for you and the baby, but it's not good for your nipples. By day three or four when your breasts get engorged with milk, you will have painful, chapped, even bloody nipples. If you use your body as a human pacifier, to satisfy your baby's sucking instincts, then when your milk does come in, your nipples will most likely be raw.

Women have very different responses to the first time their milk does come in. It can be mildly uncomfortable, or as one mother said, "I could feel my fillings tingle." When your breast milk first comes in, you may experience some pain as your breasts swell in size. If you apply cold compresses, you will relieve some of the discomfort while also slowing down the entry of milk. Warm compresses will increase the milk flow, but may make you feel worse. Once the swelling is reduced and a week or so has passed, you can use the warmth of compresses or even a shower to encourage *more* milk flow—especially if tension is getting in the way of production.

I suggest that in the first two or three days after your baby is born you attempt to put her to your breast every two to three hours, or when she wakes, for about five to ten minutes on a side, regardless of whether you are yet producing milk.

You need to be aware that some babies don't wake up very often the first week and may even be difficult to arouse. Although that may sound like a blessing, in fact a few of these babies are actually a little dehydrated—especially if their room is dry or overheated. How do you know if you are dealing with a dehydrated baby? In general, by the fourth day your baby should feed between six and ten times a day or every two to four hours. If you have a baby who does not feed at least six times a day, consider waking her a little earlier to get in an extra feeding. She should have several wet diapers a day. If diapers are wet before she falls asleep, everything is most likely fine. If, on the other hand, the baby's diapers are dry most of the day, contact your pediatrician and *wake* your baby to feed more often. Don't slap her feet or pinch her skin to wake her. Instead, undress your sleeping child completely and lay her on a flat surface such as the bed. That will usually startle her awake. Once she's up, nurse her while she is still naked except for a diaper; she's more likely to stay awake this way than if she's all swaddled, cozy, and warm against your breast.

During those first few days leave your blouse or robe open as often as you can so air and light will get to your nipples and they will begin to toughen up. To help toughen them, sit about one foot away from the warmth of a regular lightbulb and fan the air with your hands toward your breast. This will help you to better withstand the pressure and suction of the baby's mouth when your milk is finally produced and your baby sucks. I don't recommend putting ointments or gels on your nipples. They taste lousy and they're hard to wipe off without actually recracking and hurting your nipples.

LENGTH OF FEEDINGS

Some breast-feeding specialists suggest you let the baby suck for as long as she wants to. The reason for this is that the fat and the milk's immune properties increase in concentration as the length of the feedings increase. However, the greatest quantity of milk is generated early in the feed and with time the feeds will get longer. I'm firmly opposed to letting brand-new newborns nurse for as long as they want to. You will irritate your nipples, you will be exhausted, and you'll barely know where one feed ends and the next begins. Frustration and sheer exhaustion combine to cause many women to give up breast-feeding altogether, and they often feel guilty in the process.

I suggest that after the third or fourth day you set yourself a goal of ten to fifteen minutes on each side whether your baby is sucking actively or just "fooling around" on the breast, and try again at least every three hours unless the baby demands more. Then set yourself a minimum limit of at least 1½ hours from the start of one feed to the start of the next. This will ensure your baby's getting plenty of nutrition while you are getting plenty of breaks from nursing. You should understand that your breasts never completely empty out like a bottle. In fact, you are *constantly* making milk, just not always in large quantities. It takes about an hour between feedings for your breasts to have enough milk to be "pumpable" again.

After two weeks or so, once the baby is latching on and

sucking well, she can extract about 90 percent of the milk in the first three to five minutes of sucking. Even at the beginning she is very efficient at feeding, taking two or three sucks and then dozing off. If she seems to still be hungry, then switch back to the first side if she doesn't stop sucking. When do you stop? I can answer that question with another question: For how long are you comfortable being attached to the baby? After the first few weeks your nipples will be tough enough to handle even twenty minutes on a side.

Even a newborn baby needs *time* to digest. If you feed your baby for very long periods, with one feed beginning shortly after the last, you are inviting a baby version of indigestion. When your baby stops feeding, a lot of digestive activity begins. If you could see into their little stomachs after eating, you'd witness many digestive enzymes pouring out to do their job.

If, before one and a half hours from the last feed, your baby seems hungry again, give her one of three things: your finger, her finger, or a pacifier. I don't recommend that you give the newborn baby a bottle of formula or water. If you want to fully establish breast-feeding, you don't want to give the baby any other liquid as it may reduce the inspiration to breast-feed. I generally don't suggest using bottles of water unless there is a specific need—i.e., dehydration or hard stools. If you give the baby water—which doesn't satisfy hunger—you are taking time away from breast-feeding. You could even make breast-feeding more difficult, since it's been suggested that a baby can become confused between the rubber nipple and the maternal nipple. Babies don't really get confused, but they do go for what is easiest and it takes less effort to suck out of a bottle than a breast.

RECOMMENDED DAILY ALLOWANCES
FOR NURSING MOTHERS

NUTRIENT	NON-PREGNANT NEED	PREGNANT NEED	NURSING NEED	FOOD SOURCES
Protein	46 g	75–100 g	66–70 g	Milk, cheese, eggs, meat, grains, legumes, nuts
Calories	2100	2400	2600	Carbohydrates, fats (200–300 calories per day during the first three months after birth come from the mother's stored fat)
Minerals				
Calcium	800 mg	1200 mg	1200 mg	Milk, cheese, grains, leafy vegetables, egg yolks
Phosphorus	800 mg	1200 mg	1200 mg	Milk, cheese, lean meats
Iron	18 mg	18 mg + 30–60 mg supplement	18 mg	Liver, other meats, eggs, grain, leafy vegetables, nuts, dried fruits
Iodine	100 mcg	125 mcg	150 mcg	Iodized salt, seafood
Magnesium	300 mg	450 mg	450 mg	Nuts, soybeans, cocoa, seafood, whole grains, dried peas
Vitamins				
A	4000 IU	5000 IU	6000 IU	Butter, cream, fortified margarine, green and yellow vegetables
D	0	400 IU	400 IU	Fortified milk, fortified margarine (and sunshine)
E	12 IU	15 IU	15 IU	Vegatable oils, leafy vegetables, cereal, meat, eggs, milk
C	45 mg	60 mg	80 mg	Citrus fruits, berries, melon, tomatoes, green vegetables, potatoes
Folic acid	400 mcg	800 mcg	600 mcg	Liver, green vegetables

NUTRIENT	NON-PREGNANT NEED	PREGNANT NEED	NURSING NEED	FOOD SOURCES
B complex:				
Niacin	13 mg	15 mg	18 mg	Meat, peanuts, beans, peas
Riboflavin	1.2 mg	1.5 mg	1.9 mg	Milk, liver, grains
Thiamin	1.0 mg	1.3 mg	1.4 mg	Meat, grains
B_6	2 mg	2.5 mg	2.5 mg	Grains, liver, meat
B_{12}	3 mcg	4 mcg	4 mcg	Milk, eggs, meat, cheese

ADDING A BOTTLE

I recommend that breast-feeding mothers *do* plan to introduce a bottle to the baby's routine after the first two to three weeks. By this time, a bottle of formula or a bottle of expressed breast milk could be used once a day or once every other day. (Pumped milk keeps twenty-four hours in the refrigerator and months in the freezer.) You are adding an occasional bottle to her daily menu so that she will not turn down a bottle when it is *necessary* to give her one. You are doing this for both you and your baby—your baby will learn how to transfer her breast-feeding suck to the artificial nipple version, and you should be reassured that if you have to leave the house, your baby can still be fed.

I believe that all children should have the option of knowing how to suck and digest milk from a bottle for the purposes of survival. You may not always be available. If you don't try this rather early, your baby may reject your attempts later on.

MYTHS

- Myth: If you breast-feed, you lose weight.
- Myth: If you breast-feed, you don't lose weight.
    The truth is: It's a wash! You don't lose or gain weight because you are breast-feeding. Actually

how you fare has to do with how much you actually eat, and not how much or often you nurse.

- Myth: Breast-feeding is a form of birth control.

  This is definitely *not* true. It is not a reliable contraceptive method at all. There are women who don't have a menstrual flow while they are breast-feeding, but they can ovulate and therefore become pregnant.

- Myth: You need to drink a lot of milk.

  Wrong. You don't need to drink milk to make milk, but you do need to drink a lot of fluids. Cows eat grass and they have no problem making milk.

- Myth: Drinking beer or wine makes the milk richer.

  Current research proves this one is also wrong—although passed down through the ages. If you are more relaxed, for whatever the reason, your milk will flow in larger but not richer quantities.

- Myth: Women with big breasts have an easier time breast-feeding.

  Nothing could be farther from the truth. The size of your breasts has no impact on how much milk you make. A new mother recently told me, "I failed to breast-feed with my first child, so I don't expect to do well this time. My breasts are too small." I explained that large breasts are filled with fat and not with more mammary ducts. You have adequate breast tissue no matter what size they are.

COMMON QUESTIONS

Q: I have a cold. Do I continue to breast-feed?

A: Yes, you have the advantage over bottle-feeding mothers in that your baby is exposed not only to your germs but also to your antibodies. While you have a cold, you are also fighting it by producing immunity and it is transferred to your baby via your breast milk. (Stick to home remedies—steam, tea, and honey—to get over your cold. If you do take any medication, check it out with your doctor first. I've had to treat babies who developed side effects to over-the-counter cold pills taken by their nursing mothers.)

Q: I have been waiting nine months to have a permanent or dye my hair. Can I, now that my baby has been born?

A: It's not recommended that you have any chemical processes applied to your hair roots while you are still breast-feeding. Chemicals pass into your general body circulation and therefore get passed along to the baby as well. Some "tip" processes are thought to be all right.

Q: How can I tell if my baby is getting enough milk?

A: This is not easy to answer. Obviously there aren't any "ounce marks" on your breasts, the way there are on a bottle. If your baby is urinating and making stool, she is getting enough milk. (See Chapter 10, "Your Baby's Health") Remember, at the end of the first two weeks of life, all we expect is that the baby regain the ounces she lost and weigh in at her birth weight once again.

BOTTLE-FEEDING

Advantages

If you are bottle-feeding, you feed less often than breast-feeding moms—about six times a day. You will be less physically tied down to your baby and someone else can easily do the feeding. In addition, your body should return to its prepregnancy state more quickly.

Bottles are also handy because you can take them anywhere and you can tell just how much the baby is getting. In the first two weeks they may drink anywhere from a half ounce to four ounces at each feeding. Some babies benefit from the higher caloric quantity of bottled milk, and seem more satisfied than after breast-feeding. (They tend to sleep for longer periods of time, and they gain weight a little faster.) Modern formulas are otherwise quite similar to breast milk in fats, protein, and carbohydrates. Most of today's formulas contain adequate amounts of vitamins. (If your formula is a concentrate or powder, find out if fluoride is in your local water supply. If there is you should not use additional fluoride supplements because too much fluoride can be a problem. Ask your doctor.)

Disadvantages

A major disadvantage is how bottle-feeding makes some mothers feel. There is a sense that moms who really care breast-feed. There is a popular book called *The Womanly Art of Breastfeeding,* which could lead a bottle-feeding mother to think she is somehow "unwomanly." Some new mothers feel that if they bottle-feed they are depriving their baby of a bonding experience. We've all seen those beautiful pictures of nursing mothers. However, there is nothing to stop you from bottle-feeding while you are holding your almost naked baby against your own naked chest. Fathers can do that as well and have the pleasure of skin-to-skin bonding.

Even though it is true that bottle-fed babies do not get the immune component of breast milk, whole generations of healthy babies have been raised on bottle feedings.

It's also more expensive to bottle-feed, and you have to buy and stock up on the necessary supplies.

Getting Started

- Your baby will be offered prepared formula in the hospital. The formula the hospital uses is usually the one the doctor will recommend. If your baby has problems digesting the formula—irritability, rashes, painful watery stools—you may need a change in formula. (*Never* change the formula unless you have discussed the change with your doctor. There are differences—for example, soy-based formulas tend to constipate, while predigested formulas loosen stools. They are not interchangeable.) Inter-

estingly, we know that babies have a sense of taste, but
we don't know that much about it. They will sometimes
spit out or refuse a particular formula, so you may have to
switch to one your baby prefers. There is also the slight
risk of feeding baby spoiled formula, so always taste what
you offer.

- In general, bottle-feeding is easier today than it was for
  our mothers. It's no longer necessary to make your own
  formula, or to boil the water unless you live somewhere
  where the well water is not clean. We *do not* sterilize bottles or nipples anymore either. You don't even need to
  warm the bottles—room temperature is probably perfect
  —and even a cold bottle is fine at three in the morning.
  (Studies show that the less time the baby is screaming
  and waiting for you to warm the bottle, the better all
  around.)
- The type of nipple the baby prefers often depends on
  what he is comfortable with from the beginning. There
  are orthodontic-shaped nipples, and there is reasonable
  evidence that they are easier for the baby to suck milk
  from without getting air in. But there is no solid evidence
  that it makes any difference to the ultimate orthodontia
  of the baby. Most hospitals do start on "O" nipples, but
  any brand is fine. I prefer silicone because they are clear,
  but they are often harder to find. Latex nipples are nota-
  ble for breaking down and getting gummy, so keep extras
  on hand. Some problems which arise with bottle-feeding
  are very easy to fix. For example, one mother came in
  with a crying baby, and we soon discovered there was no
  hole in the nipple. Sometimes *you* have to make the hole.
- I prefer clear plastic to glass bottles because of the possibility of glass shattering. The type of bottle you use is not
  as important as *how* it's held. Try not to let air get into
  the nipple. Some new bottles have an angled design so
  that air cannot get into the nipple. Always hold the bottle; *never* prop it up. It's both physically and psychologi-

cally dangerous. Your baby could gag and choke. (If you lay her down with her bottle and the bottle drops partially out of her mouth, she may experience both frustration and discomfort by sucking milk and air.) It also lacks intimacy and is emotionally depriving: you are missing the opportunity for mother/baby eye contact and the relationship of trust which develops.

I also prefer bottles that allow your baby to suck without completely back-tilting the head. Recent evidence has it that keeping the head in a neutral or slightly flexed position may reduce the incidence of ear infections. Bottles with an angled neck, straw insert, or disposable liner address this very neatly.

If you are interrupted while feeding, take the bottle out of the baby's mouth, even if she cries. When bottle-feeding try sitting in a comfortable rocker or armchair and place pillows under your elbows. Cradle your baby close to your breast with her head held a little higher than the rest of her body. Keep the bottle tipped so that air doesn't appear in the nipple. (If you have twins, feed them individually or lay both down on a soft pillow and hold one bottle in each hand. There are four sets of triplets in my practice, and they are fed in round-robin fashion—two get to feed, and one gets to watch.)

BURPING

All babies need to be burped. Burp a bottle-fed newborn after every ounce of formula; stop between breasts to burp a breast-fed baby. Just put the baby over your shoulder and pat firmly in the middle of her back, not near the top of the chest. Give up after five minutes. Most babies burp spontaneously if you lay them down: put a little pressure on your baby's back and you may find a little spit-up under her cheek. You

Several burping positions can be tried, but a burp
is not always necessary. If baby is happy and calm
during feeding spend no more than a few minutes
trying to "get the air out."

may also produce a burp. If you put her in an infant
seat after feeding, her inclined posture may also aid in
digestion.

GROWTH SPURTS

Babies tend to grow in sudden spurts and not gradually. At
about three weeks and again at six weeks, when these spurts
are likely to occur, you may notice that both bottle- and
breast-fed babies start to feed voraciously. This is not commonly known, and just about every mother in my practice calls
me to discuss her suddenly ravenous baby.

If you are bottle-feeding, then let the baby take the lead.
She really won't take too much, and even if she did, she would
eventually spit up, which would cause no harm. If you are
breast-feeding, go back to feeding every two hours. In a short
amount of time your breasts will have more milk per feeding.

Another comfortable position that helps baby to
burp or pass gas is with the baby lying across your
lap.

In order for the quantity of breast milk to increase to meet the
needs of your growing baby, there must be times when your
baby feeds voraciously and frequently. This doesn't mean you
won't have enough milk. Your baby's vigorous sucking is a signal to the mammary glands to produce more milk and then
feeding frequency will slow up again, because *per* feeding there
will be more milk available. This is truly a supply/demand system. Adding a formula bottle at this time is exactly what *not*
to do if you want to continue to exclusively breast-feed. After a
few days, and within a week at the most, the baby should settle
down again to feeding every three to four hours.

This may be the month the baby will gain two and a half to
three pounds instead of one or two. The typical baby gains
four to eight ounces a week. Breast-fed babies gain about one
pound a month; bottle-fed babies gain a little more. You want
the baby to have doubled her birth weight by six months, although many bottle-fed babies double their birth weight
sooner.

This is another good burping position, in which
the baby sits upright on your lap while you pat
firmly on the middle of her back.

DEMAND FEEDING OR SCHEDULED FEEDS?

I suggest you feed your newborn when she cries and nothing
else will soothe her. With few exceptions, feed the baby when
she's hungry.

   If you are the kind of person who likes to follow a schedule,
to some extent you may succeed in imposing a feeding routine
on your baby, but it won't be as predictable as you'd like. In
fact, it shouldn't be rigid, because you can't expect your baby
to suppress her appetite or to eat when she's not hungry just
because four hours have passed. On the other hand, if you
want the baby to tell you when to feed her, you have to be
sensitive to her signals of hunger. It's not always easy to tell,
since most of what babies do at this age is cry. Sticking a
nipple in your baby's mouth every time she cries will at least
temporarily satisfy most needs other than pain, but not every
cry is a cry for food. (See Chapter 7, "The Crying Baby.") You
don't want to teach her that eating is the solution to all of

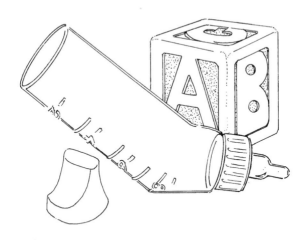

Use bottles that are designed to reduce the amount
of air the baby can swallow.

life's discomforts. Here's a good rule of thumb: If your baby
has been well fed within the past one and a half hours, you can
assume you are *not* dealing with a hungry baby.

Some people believe if you give formula late in the evening,
you will have a baby who will sleep through the night. Sorry.
There's no link between sleeping through the night and late
feeding. I advise parents not to be hemmed in by the need for
consistency. (As I remind parents, "Consistency is the hobgob-
lin of small minds.") Babies don't mind if one day you give the
formula feeding at two in the afternoon and next day at two in
the morning.

If your baby is sleeping, unless you have specific instructions
from the doctor (maybe the baby was premature or under-
weight), *never wake a sleeping baby*. If you're lucky enough to
have a baby who sleeps five hours through the night, just
smile. And get some sleep.

GAS

Babies have gas from day one, but to differing degrees. Not all babies have pain; some just produce gas painlessly, though often noisily. The cause of it is the establishment of normal bacteria in your baby's gut. This is also why the notion of boiling bottles is nonsense. We are not sterile to begin with. If we were, we could not digest our food properly. Our intestines need to maintain a symbiotic relationship with normal bacteria. These bacteria participate in the process of digestion and produce gas. Pain is caused when gas expands and the intestines are stretched. There is a period of adjustment to the various kinds of bacteria vying to set up shop in the proper proportions—just enough *E. coli*, just enough enterococcus, etc. In that battle, there are bound to be periods of distress.

There are other causes of gas production which are

not so benign. Some bottle-fed babies are plagued by gas as a result of poor digestion of milk. The major ingredient in most common formulas is cow's milk, which has a sugar and a protein that not all people can handle. Many adults, in fact, have intolerance to the sugar in cow's milk—in addition, when you pass undigested sugar into the lower intestine, it's very gas-producing. Sometimes it is necessary to switch formulas. Breast-fed babies also have gas, but usually to a lesser degree.

You can help your baby to deal with painful gas, which usually lasts for only a few seconds or minutes, in several ways. If it comes on rather frequently, then bowel distension is probably what is causing the pain —and the gas is "stuck." You can actually hear the gut rumbling and see the baby kicking. Put the baby in motion: into an infant seat, swing, sling, or a stroller rocked back and forth. Even just hoisting the baby up on your shoulder may help, because gas moves and will, with motion and gravity, "fall" in one direction or the other. Or you could put the baby belly-down on a hard surface with a soft covering, and rock her from side to side while putting some pressure on her back with the palm of your hand. As you flatten her belly, it helps to roll the gas along. According to folklore, feeding certain kinds of teas to your baby like camomile, anise, or fennel work well, because they absorb or break up the gas. Brew a weak solution using equal parts tea and cold tap water. There are several drugs on the market which are simethicone-based. I don't recommend them, because they rarely work and they can sedate the baby unnaturally.

THE PSYCHOLOGY OF FEEDING: INCLUDING FATHER

There is little that bonds a relationship more than having the responsibility for another person's sustenance. Feeding is supportive in the most basic way. It's not uncommon for fathers to feel left out of the incredibly intense relationship that is evolving between mother and baby even when the mother is bottle-feeding. It's not just nursing mothers who exclude fathers, but certainly breast-feeding accentuates the issue. The husband may be looking longingly at his wife, whose breasts no longer seem to "belong" to him, and at his baby, who doesn't seem to need him much either. It's also often uncomfortable for most women to resume sexual relations with their husbands while they are breast-feeding—their breasts are leaking milk, and often hurt. All of this may delay husband and wife becoming a couple again. And now there appears to be a *new* couple in the house—Mom and the baby.

In general, there are two reasons why mothers have problems with sharing the feeding—particularly breast-feeding mothers:

1. Some women have heard if they use a relief bottle of any sort, the baby will have nipple confusion—he will be confused between the action needed to suck on a breast nipple and the action needed to suck on a rubber nipple. The truth is that very little confusion actually occurs as long as you don't repeatedly switch back and forth. If it's only done once a day, or you've already established breast-feeding over the first two or three weeks, there is usually no problem. I can't recall ever seeing a case of true nipple confusion under these conditions. Obviously if you are bottle-feeding, there is no confusion at all.

2. The second reason strikes right at the heart of the matter. Many new mothers don't want to lose control of the nurturing experience. Breast-feeding mothers are not bonded any closer to their babies than bottle-feeding mothers, but they often believe that breast milk is superior and it's

something only they can really do. I've heard mothers say with pride, "My baby wants nothing but me." It's a badge of honor some mothers wear: "Nothing has passed his lips except breast milk." This can easily cause fathers to withdraw and even fade out of the immediate picture. As one dad in a new fathers' group lamented, "I don't have breasts. What can *I* do?"

Similarly, bottle-feeding mothers are often possessive: it's as if they think the hand that holds the bottle "owns" the baby! Some moms feel they have learned all the tricks of the bottle-feeding trade and are a little jealous if Dad too easily steps right in and succeeds.

• Fathers should be encouraged to participate in feeding in a meaningful way. In the past, the fathers used to be the person who fed the baby a bottle in the middle of the night. Breast-feeding mothers may let their husbands feed the baby a bottle of pumped breast milk at that late hour. I find that there is something very illogical and unfair about that. It's not quite right to expect your husband to happily bond at two in the morning when *he* is likely to be exhausted. You are really tossing him the crumbs of feeding by giving him the least desirable time. I suggest that new mothers understand that fathers also get to bond when they get to feed. Letting him feed the baby is an important step in bringing your threesome together and closing the gaps between you and your mate. Make a place for him. Now.

(Actually, there is a new, very "nineties" device which allows fathers to practically breast-feed. It's a bra with two sacks and nipples on the end. The father slips the device on after filling it with milk, and he can "breast-feed." I personally think this is carrying things a little too far, but there are fathers who say it has helped them feel part of the experience.)

- A father can participate in feeding even if the mother wants to exclusively breast-feed and is really uncomfortable with adding a bottle. One lovely way is for the father to hold his wife while she feeds the baby. Often it's in bed, usually late in the evening or early in the morning. Make it cozy and meaningful. This can be very rewarding if you are willing to let your partner be a part of it.

- If your husband does feed the baby, then you have to let him do it his way. Some mothers feel they are the expert, the professional, and the husband is sort of an amateur. Yes, it is difficult to watch someone who appears inept, who fumbles around with a bottle, so that maybe milk even slurps down the baby's chin. The temptation is to step in and say, "No, honey, do it this way," or "Let me do it." Resist this and let the father and baby fumble on their own a little bit. They will work it out if you let them.

We know that a very special relationship does develop between the baby and the person who feeds him. Up to three months old, a baby optimally can see clearest at the distance from your arms to your eyes. That's what goes on during feeding—there is eye contact between the baby and his feeder. It makes for memories of early love, and it's truly sad when a father misses out on these moments. Later on, you'll be rewarded by the close relationship between father and child. Studies show that fathers who feed their babies play with them more as well.

COMING ATTRACTIONS

Both formula and breast milk will meet all your baby's nutritional needs until at least four months and usually until six months. (At this age, babies go for longer periods without eating.) For several good reasons, we no longer feed babies any solid food in the first few months. In the past, mothers were advised to add cereal or fruit in a pureed form and just widened the nipple to accommodate it in the bottle. We were sneaking in extra calories. We now know that obesity has roots in early overfeeding. Worse, these foods just aren't meant to be eaten by a baby who can't sit up. The process of digestion isn't ready yet, and sucking coordination is not in place. The ability to gum, swallow, and digest cereal or carrots kicks in between four and six months. Also before that time, the body recognizes these foods as foreign and may develop antibody responses which result in a variety of allergies and an allergic skin condition called eczema. Juice is not as good as the fruit it came from and should be avoided as it adds useless sugary calories and may even harm the growing baby teeth.

If you are breast-feeding, you may have questions about when to stop. This is a very personal issue. Your body will respond to demand for at least the first five to six months. In very few cases does the natural cycle of breast-feeding start to turn itself off earlier. There are many ways to part-wean, particularly if you want to go back to work. Remember that greater than 80 percent of immunity is transferred to the baby in the first three months, so that three months is often the point when mothers do choose to wean.

CHAPTER *6*

· ·

Sleeping

A mother recently came into my office and showed me a card she had received congratulating her on the birth of her son. It read: "I know you will be able to rise to the occasion . . . about eight times a night." She was much too tired to laugh. The truth is the card was right on target: sleepless nights and infants are a fact of most new parents' lives. So when this new mom asked me (as hundreds of mothers have before her), "How do I get my three-week-old son to sleep through the night?" I answered, "You can't." What you *can* expect is to be up two to four times a night.

Infants don't sleep through the night the way adults do. They may sleep as many as twelve to eighteen hours per day, but they do it in small bursts. All of us are capable of waking up many times during the night, yet we rarely do. Our brain waves take us in and out of different levels of consciousness, sleep being one of those levels. Babies generally go through the same phases but more frequently. Every three to four hours they alternate between sleeping lightly, deeply, lightly, deeply —on some of these occasions they will become aware of the sensation of hunger, wake up fully, cry, and get fed. Then they sleep lightly, deeply, lightly, deeply again, and this pattern repeats itself some six to ten times a day.

Babies also do not respond the same way adults do to darkness and light. Research shows that light responsiveness starts at about five or six months of age. Newborns can sleep in bright light and be wide awake in the dark. I'll get frantic calls from a mother: "My baby is all mixed up. He doesn't know night from day and seems to sleep more during the day and less at night." The baby isn't confused and is unlikely to turn into a permanent night owl; he is just following his own time clock, which is different from ours. Night and day sleeping are not distinguishable for a newborn. You can't *fool* a newborn into thinking it's night and time to go to sleep. You just have to live with it, and sleep when your baby sleeps. Most new mothers have no problem falling asleep if only they allow themselves to. Similarly, just as they can sleep in light, babies can usually sleep in a noisy environment. You don't need to whisper. You can usually safely assume that baby's sleep is independent of the noise level around them.

Babies don't have sleep problems—their parents do. There is *no* good reason for infants to sleep straight through the night except to have happier parents in the morning. In the pursuit of this happiness, tired moms have been known to try just about anything. But it's a myth, for instance, that giving a baby cereal in his bottle at night will fill him up and keep him down or that a breast-feeding mother who drinks wine will lull the baby into a lengthier sleep. (I say, to the former, cereal can cause indigestion and lead to more sleep problems, and to the latter, wine can actually agitate babies.)

There's probably no topic that hits a nerve quite like babies and sleeping. We can make jokes about it, the way the greeting card did, but there is just no getting around it: your baby needs you when he wakes up, but at the same time you need your sleep. Your newborn will not sleep through the night and neither will you. For most adults sleep deprivation is almost crippling. (Just ask any medical intern or resident.) Many moms tell me it makes them weep with frustration and Dad absolutely has to do some night patrol.

Unfortunately there are no shortcuts to lengthening your infant's sleeping sessions at this early age. In part this is because babies have very different eating patterns from grown-ups. They don't have the stomach capacity to take in large quantities of food and they need nourishment at regular intervals around the clock. In fact, if you are lucky enough to have one of those rare infants who does sleep for long periods, your doctor may advise you to wake him to feed—particularly if he was premature or if his weight gain is insufficient.

Some good news is that breast-fed babies tend to fall asleep easily after feeding—in fact, while they are feeding. The bad news is they wake up about every two to three hours because they are hungry again. On the other hand, bottle-fed babies can take in a larger load of calories per ounce of milk (breast milk has fewer calories per ounce) and frequently sleep about three to four hours at a time.

Strong warning: Do not leave the bottle in your baby's mouth after he falls asleep. You don't want him to become accustomed to drinking while sleeping; it's dangerous, since he may choke, and it can also lead to tooth decay.

When they do sleep, babies can be put in any one of three positions: on the front, on the back, or on the side. There is literature to support the superiority of each of these three positions. I'm on the staff of three hospitals. One puts baby on the side, one on the back, and, until recently, one on the belly. Each hospital claims its choice is based on "solid scientific grounds." Obviously, there is no one perfect position. The American Academy of Pediatrics recently released a statement which said that babies should not be placed on their belly. There is a concern that you might place your baby on a *soft* surface and his face could sink in. It's been suggested you put baby on his side. It's been my experience that the optimum position is still on his stomach, because on his back there is the increased risk of the baby spitting up and then swallowing and choking on the vomit. I still say that the safest position is on the belly provided the baby is on a firm surface. Side-lying or belly-down are the positions which most closely approximates the womb—knees up, neck flexed, and arms tucked in.

BABY'S BEDROOM

The first few weeks of your baby's life, it's probably safest and most convenient to have him sleeping very close to you. The baby wakes often and it's easier to get him from the side of the bed than from the next room. It makes the most sense to put your newborn in a bassinet, or cradle, or even a carriage next to your bed when you get home from the hospital.

The bassinet should be small enough so that the baby feels securely surrounded, yet large enough so when he stretches his arms, they are not hitting the sides. The typical bassinet is 18 inches across and 30 inches in length—and baby is approximately 20 inches long or 25 inches with his arms stretched up. (By the time the baby is about two months old, he should be out of a bassinet and into a crib. Some babies turn over at three months and would be in danger of falling out.)

Finding the right place for a baby to sleep may sound a little bit like replaying "Goldilocks": this one may be too hard, that one too soft, and finally you'll find the one that is *just right*. The mattress doesn't have to be hard and stiff—just firm enough so baby can't sink into it. There can be a problem with homemade and makeshift sleeping areas. (For example, some parents create a sleeping area by placing a pillow inside an enclosed playpen. Unfortunately, the softness of the pillow might allow the baby's head to sink into it and create a pocket in which the baby might suffocate.) Make sure the mattress isn't made of animal hair, because some babies will have an allergic reaction to it.

Put a cotton sheet on the mattress because babies tend not to be allergic to it and cotton seems to be more comfortable for them. Babies don't need pillows, even though pillows are sold to you in blanket sets. If he sleeps on a pillow, he may bend his neck in a way that could make it harder for him to breathe freely. You can, however, have baby bumpers if they are narrow and tightly secured to the sides of the crib. The surface baby sleeps on should be free of all snaps, buttons, and zippers. Every night you should check the crib for anything that could have fallen in—babies tend to grasp whatever is there and pull it right to their mouth. Blankets, when necessary, should be lightweight. In general a baby's *sleep outfit* should be his blanket, not a heavy cover that he might get tangled in.

DEVELOPING HEALTHY SLEEP HABITS

For the first few weeks, there is nothing more reassuring to the baby than physical contact. But after that, it is time to think of separating yourself from him just as he is about to fall into deep sleep. I've heard mothers in my new mothers' groups complain, "Now, what do I do? I've finally got the baby to sleep and *I* can't move." When I ask "why?" they answer, "Because I'm *under* the baby." (Yes, you should try to sleep when the baby is asleep but not necessarily while attached to each other!)

If you help your baby fall asleep in his bassinet or crib, he will be able to do it on his own much sooner. Your baby can eventually learn to put himself to sleep, but you can't expect him to go "cold turkey" from rocking on your nice warm body to just being put down in a crib still awake. When the baby is starting to fall asleep—his eyelids are fluttering—carry him to his crib before he is fast asleep.

When you put him down in his crib, the last thing he remembers before falling asleep will be the first thing he searches for during the night when his sleep pattern lightens. If that last thing was your arms or a bottle in his mouth and he can't easily replace it, he will invariably cry. What you would like him to be remembering is the nice comfortable mattress.

After the first month or two, if he is still sleeping next to you in your room, you increase the chances of waking up your baby. You tend to sleep lightly as a new parent; every movement of the baby makes you get up and think, "My baby is up, I should be up." No, you shouldn't. You will tend to feed each other's alert mechanisms. Here's a common scenario: The baby makes a little noise, and you lean over to see him and rustle the sheets, and he wakes up and cries. Instead, I suggest you lie still when you hear that little noise and he will probably go right back to sleep. It's not fair to wake him at his first movement.

Tip: If you use a pacifier to put your child to sleep, remember to remove it once he's nodded off. Again, don't get into the dangerous habit of giving your baby a bottle in his crib: not only will he look for the bottle each time he wakens, but we now know that it can harm the baby's teeth and he can choke on the fluid held in his mouth.

SLEEP TIPS

- If your baby is very jittery and has trouble sleeping, try swaddling him. Sometimes being wrapped up snugly will encourage relaxation and sleep. (To swaddle a baby: Turn one corner of a blanket down, off center; put the baby on the blanket a little to one side; wrap the shorter end around his body and then fold the bottom corner up; now take the long end and wrap it all the way around him.)
- It's nice to have a mobile, music, or maybe one of the specially designed stuffed animals which simulate "uterine" sounds.
- Try holding a cloth diaper while you are nursing or feeding, and then put that cloth diaper in the crib *along* with baby. The smell the cloth acquires from your body, plus just the association of it being there in your arms, is sometimes enough to make baby sleep. (See Chapter 7, "The Crying Baby," for more on transitional objects.)
- If your baby doesn't sleep easily during the day, put him down for *little* catnaps on your belly. Or he can even sleep

in a Snugli—this way at least your hands are free and your baby loves the motion. You can try a swing, as long as you are in attendance at all times.

- You can create a warm cozy napping place by using a hot water bottle that is well wrapped in insulated material such as terry cloth. Fill it three-quarters full with luke-warm water. Put the baby on his side and mold the water bottle to his belly. It gives a nice sensation of warmth and motion and can even be helpful in other circumstances. (See "Gas," p. 97, and "Colic," p. 119.)

- It's very important to remember that at this age the baby should *not* be left in his crib to cry. If he can't fall asleep after about five minutes, then he belongs back in your arms.

- The baby should have only pleasant associations with his crib. Don't ever use the crib as a "jail" or put him in it as an angry or punishing gesture. The crib will be your friend for the first two years—don't transform it into your enemy.

NAPPING

One of the ways a baby passes his time is napping. Napping doesn't have to occur in the traditional sleeping-at-night position in his crib—it can occur anywhere. You may even be lucky enough to have a baby who naps when you go out for a walk.

One of the ways to help your baby to nap is to put him in a cradle. I know they are not in vogue right now, but I've always liked cradles, and you already have a cradle if you think about it: you have your arms. There is no reason in the first few months, es-pecially during the day, why you can't sit in a rocking chair with the baby napping on you. He can even rock himself into a nap in a rocking infant seat. The slight-est motion by the baby causes more motion. You could also put the baby down for a nap in his stroller and push it back and forth over a doorsill. Some strollers and most larger carriages have their own spring action.

You can expect your newborn to spend many periods a day "catnapping." These periods can range from ten minutes to as long as two hours. Some babies eat, are alert, then get irritable and maybe eat again, and finally sleep for a short while. Sometimes there may be one or two periods a day when they sleep for two to three hours and then they may not nap at all.

As the baby gets older, sleep will become more normalized. Some babies will nap briefly twice a day, while others take just one long nap. It's very common for babies to take one nap in the morning and then an afternoon siesta and finally sleep through the night once they reach four to six months.

COMING ATTRACTIONS

The biggest changes in baby's sleeping patterns will occur at about five months, or when the infant has doubled his birthweight. It is no longer necessary to feed the baby in the middle of the night. In addition, his sleep/wake brain wave patterns are such that he doesn't awaken as easily and he can now sleep for increasingly longer periods.

If you follow these suggestions, you should be able to help your baby sleep through the night:

You can't expect to put your baby in his crib and he'll just give up waking for sleeping. You need to let the baby know that it's bedtime: you might dim the lights, pull the shades, and generally quiet the house. Some babies at five to six months do need pitch-dark, and you may have to buy blackout shades for early-morning sunlight. You are sending a message that it's now sleeptime. You might try saying out loud: "Now we're going to sleep, little one."

You want to develop a bedtime ritual which is different from naptime. Have a firm idea in your mind how long it should last. Babies can tune in to your vibrations. If you don't have an end point to the ritual, your baby won't have an end point either. The ritual might be two lullabies, one cuddle-kiss, and a trip around the room saying good night to the various stuffed animals and dolls. After a while the baby will come to expect that ritual. Do it over and over. Don't worry—your baby won't get bored.

When the ritual is over, put the baby in his crib and rub or pat his back for a few moments. Turn on a record, wind up a musical mobile, anything the baby likes to listen to; or maybe face a favorite picture toward him for him to look at as he closes his eyes. Remember it's hard for your baby to just let go of you, so don't be surprised if he whimpers or whines a little. It's perfectly normal for him to experience a little bit of distress as he gives up being awake—to a baby this represents the ultimate separation from you.

If your baby continues to cry, wait five to ten minutes—the time it should take for your baby to fall asleep. Ten minutes is about as long as your newborn can keep his image of you in his head without really panicking; this is also about as long as most parents can reasonably be expected to tolerate the noise. If the crying doesn't stop, then you need to return to the room at about five-minute intervals. I don't believe in letting a baby just cry endlessly. (One popular child-care book advocates that parents wait increasingly longer periods to check up on baby: this usually makes the baby scream louder and longer, because that will increase the chances of your coming back. I have had parents who followed that advice tell me that police have appeared at their door in the middle of the night, because neighbors feared for the safety of the baby!)

If you do go back in, *less is best*. Say almost nothing. (*"Shh. Go back to sleep."*) Briefly reassure the baby you are there. Don't give him a bottle, and never pick the baby up unless you want him to get up. (Maybe your husband just got home and hasn't seen the baby.) If you reward the baby for waking up by playing with him, he has no good reason to go back to sleep. As long as the baby continues to cry, you continue to check in at five-minute intervals.

What if your baby goes to bed easily at eight in the evening, but then wakes up at two in the morning? Simple: You are in the same situation you would be in if he'd had trouble going to sleep in the first place. Again, do as little as possible when you enter the room. Don't reinforce his waking up and he can be taught to go back to sleep.

It should take about a week to get a five- to six-month-old baby to adapt to a more adult sleeping pattern and to be convinced that going to sleep and staying asleep can be a pleasant experience.

CHAPTER 7

The Crying Baby

Except for the very *first* cry a baby makes when she is born, there is no question that the sound of a baby crying seems to pierce right through your body. New mothers may think that they are supposed to automatically know what each cry means. No one can. At conventions, pediatricians have been asked to listen to tapes of crying babies, and they can't guess what each baby wants any more than you can. A new mom recently said, "Dr. Paula, I feel like I'm supposed to be able to 'read' Sam and know what he wants when he cries," but babies aren't such open books. It would be wonderful if infants were delivered with translation books to interpret their cries!

The bottom line is that your baby has virtually no other way of communicating except through her cry. They do talk, if you can understand their language. I like to think that babies are born singing. You and your baby form a "duet" from the moment of birth. At the very beginning some mothers respond to their baby's voice by repeating or mimicking the sound, and the baby usually responds to this "conversation" by repeating the sound back. Other mothers try to interpret the baby's sound and assume it has some particular meaning—maybe it's a cry of hunger or distress, and they respond not with a sound but with an action.

There are definite connections between our babies and our

bodies—again, there is that invisible cord. Within hours of birth, some mothers can even distinguish their own baby's cry from that of other babies. It's been observed that breast-feeding mothers will produce *more* milk to the cries of their own baby, although they can produce milk to the cries of other babies as well. When babies cry, it's a communication meant just for you.

A newborn baby's cry varies mostly only in volume—they have little control over the pitch or tone until about two to three months. Some babies are equipped with high-pitched cries which many adults find irritating. As you might expect, the bigger the newborn, the louder the cry. Preemies have a very quiet cry; they literally don't have the strength to generate much volume.

I tell new mothers: Don't worry, you will definitely be able to hear your baby when she cries, which is why I don't recommend electronic baby monitors. Unless you live in a very large house, monitors are unnecessary and can even be intrusive. Over the years, I've observed that a woman who was once a sound sleeper will wake at the slightest stir after she becomes a mother. There are good reasons why monitors are a bad idea. The monitor alerts you too quickly to the subtle, small sounds a baby makes (i.e., rolling side to side, stretching, rubbing against the sheets). Often a monitor transforms a little sigh into a big cry.

I'm not trying to discourage mothers from responding to their babies, but not every sound a baby makes is a sound of distress. Your baby is learning that she *has* a voice and she needs to exercise it privately. If you respond too quickly to every sound she makes, she will have no opportunity to figure out what sounds she can make. Don't run in at every amplified whisper; it's startling to her if you dash in every time she makes a peep.

Monitors also create a false sense of security—as if the monitor is really standing guard over your baby. By mistakenly believing that you will be alerted if anything *is* wrong, you may not go in every once in a while just to check on the baby. I tell new parents it's better to peek in occasionally if that makes you feel better than to hover over the microphone of the monitor.

WHY BABIES CRY

Babies cry for a variety of reasons, but it is always an expression of some need. They can be hungry, tired, wet, sick, uncomfortable, frightened, or even lonely.

A common mistake parents make is to assume that every time their baby cries, she must be hungry, and they are too quick to respond with a feeding. I recently had a new mother tearfully complain to me that she feels as if she's become a kind of living bottle—nursing her baby nonstop. This grown woman has allowed herself to be held hostage by a seven-pound crying baby. (Whenever I ask parents, "Why are you feeding the baby all the time?" the answer I get back is, "Because the baby is crying and she stops when I feed her." That may be true, but it doesn't mean the baby is hungry.)

Right then and there I talked to this mother, as I've talked to countless other parents, about *limit setting*. Many mothers express the view that if they could anticipate every need their child had and prevent their child from feeling any discomfort, they would. Well, I wouldn't. You will be permanently doomed to failure if you try. And it's not even good for your baby. She is a growing independent human being who deserves the right to learn how to communicate her needs. We mistakenly feel if we only knew what every cry meant, we would be able to create better, happier people. But even happy, healthy adults cry and feel discomfort and pain. So the mother who is feeding her child all the time must develop a new way of thinking to replace the old one. "It's not likely my child is hungry again after feeding well only twenty minutes ago. So I'll set a limit in my mind. For at least an hour, I'll try not to feed her again. I will try to figure out what else I can do to comfort her."

You are teaching the baby a very important lesson: She is half of a communicating team. The baby holds some of the responsibility, albeit a limited one. You are both trying to understand each other and you each have to expend some effort. Although they don't carry on the sophisticated internal dialogue of the adorable baby in *Look Who's Talking*, they can communicate. They learn very quickly, for example, that crying brings certain results. What a wonderful lesson!

It's equally important to understand when *not* to set limits. Up to about three months, you do have to respond quickly to a crying baby. (But remember that "respond" doesn't translate into "feed.") You should pick up the baby. Some babies stop crying when they see an adult smile or when they are held very close. Feeling your touch, smelling your perfume, hearing you sing, listening as you wind up her mobile—all of those can quiet a crying baby. A baby who isn't attended to when she cries just cries more, not less. (If Grandma complains that you're going to spoil the baby, answer, "Fruit spoils; not infants.") And most parents find it more painful to listen to the crying than to pick up the baby, who can't really tell you what's bothering her.

Again, research indicates that babies who cry and are picked up cry less on the average than babies who are left to cry. As the baby grows a little older, about the third month, you can set small limits. ("I think my baby can handle crying for a little while," so from the open doorway to her room you reassure her, "Don't worry, Jenny, I'll be there in a minute." And Jenny hears your voice, knows you are there, and calms down a little.)

When you do pick up the baby, always talk to her. The sooner you use language, the sooner you are coupling the feeling of comfort with the sound of comfort. ("Mommy is here.") Babies learn self-control by experiencing small doses of frustration. The goal of this particular "lesson" is to teach her to increase the length of time she can go without you. Your baby must be feeling terrific as she begins to develop her own little bag of tricks. She discovers she can soothe herself for a short while by sucking on or just looking at her fingers, by puckering up her lips, by opening and closing her eyes, or maybe by gazing at a pattern that's within a one-foot vicinity.

In fact, many crying babies just need something to suck, which is why babies find their fingers. Sucking isn't just for nutrition; it fills a neurological and psychological need as well. Now that we regularly do sonograms, we can see a baby in utero sucking on his thumb—it's part of a natural process of growth and change. Some babies have a greater need to suck than others. A pacifier is useful for some hard-core suckers— it's a good substitute for her hands—although some parents do object to the look of a "plugged-up" baby. If you *do* use pacifiers, buy them by the half-dozen. (I like to joke that there is a "Nuk monster" in everyone's home who lives under the crib and steals pacifiers.) *Never* dip a pacifier in honey and never, ever tie it around your baby's neck on a string. It's also a good idea to remove the pacifier from his mouth once he has fallen asleep.

There's a lot of trial and error in figuring out just *how* to comfort a crying baby. Go through your mental checklist: If he has recently been fed, doesn't want to suck, and his diaper isn't wet, consider that he might just want to be held and cuddled.

A baby who is being held and is *still* crying may be gassy. Try jiggling the baby, or rocking him back and forth in his stroller over a doorsill. (See Chapter 5, "Feeding," for advice.) If you hear rumbling or grumbling noises in his belly, put the baby in motion—infant seats, swings, and slings are helpful. There's even a device that mimics car motion because, as any mother will tell you, being driven around in a car is almost always a cure for a gassy baby. (This particular device was created by a pediatrician who was tired of driving around his *own* crying baby; he developed a motor which simulates the sound and sensation of a car rumbling at fifty-five miles per hour and can be attached to the bottom of a crib.) Parents have become ingenious at replicating good vibrations. Some parents put their babies in an infant seat on top of a running washing machine or dryer; others keep a vacuum cleaner running. (Some babies will calm at just the recorded sound of a vacuum cleaner! I'm not sure why this would work, but it's worth a try!)

Parents develop their own ways of calming their baby, often by singing or dancing with him. Some babies are soothed by repetitive sounds—like ocean waves. I know mothers who turn tap water on to duplicate the rushing sound of blood flow that the baby listened to while in the uterus. Other parents play relaxation tapes or lullabies, and find *themselves* nodding off. If your baby is just moody, try a change of atmosphere—he could be bothered by bright lights, odors, noise, or maybe he's just plain bored.

Of course, you must always make sure that your baby is not trying to communicate to you that he's not feeling well. That is why, if at any time your baby's cry sounds significantly different to you than it had previously, you should immediately go in and investigate. Maybe he is warm, indicating that he has a fever and you need to call the doctor. If you cannot console a baby after you've tried all else, then you still need to talk to the doctor. I will often get a call, "My baby is *still* crying. He doesn't have a fever. What could it mean?" I run through the checklist of possible solutions, and if the mother has tried them all twice and the baby is still crying, then I ask her to come in to my office. It could be a cry of pain which needs medical attention. On the other hand, if I get a call at two in the morning and the mom says, "My son has been crying for hours, he has no fever, and he only stops crying when he is on my shoulder, do you think something is wrong?," I am able to reassure her, "It's precisely because he *does* stop that you know he is all right. Just keep him on your shoulder, and for tonight try to sleep on your feet! Then we all can go back to bed."

COLIC

There are babies who cry, and then there are babies who *cry*. A baby who cries inconsolably for long periods is said to be colicky. Colic is hard to define because it's not a scientific term. No one really knows what it is, but it is definitely not a disease. Colic usually occurs between two weeks and three months of age and is associated with a cranky baby who is usually crankiest in the evening, although it can be all day. She can cry, wail, and shriek for hours at a time. Contrary to some commonly held beliefs, colic isn't caused by bottle-feeding; breast-fed babies can also get colicky. It doesn't seem to be related to feeding at all, because it is not predictable. Parents often change formulas, but it does no good. If it were related to feeding, then colic wouldn't happen primarily in the evening. (If, however, crankiness occurs *only* in relation to feeds, then check with your pediatrician—a change of formula just might help.) Even though it's not a digestive problem, I tell mothers to treat colic in much the same way you would gassiness, which means to let the baby move around. Often a mother may need to pace for hours with the baby on her in a front carrier just to achieve peace.

Some research indicates that colic occurs in the evening as a result of the body's decreased production of a hormone known as cortisol. Most of this hormone is produced in the morning, and as the day goes on, less and less is produced and our mood worsens. By the time a newborn has hit five o'clock, his cortisol level has dropped to its low point and he may experience a mood dip.

Since colic also seems to have something to do with the transition from fetal to newborn state, try to re-create the dark, fluid environment of the womb. Some people like to take the baby into the bath on their chest. (I've also prescribed warm camomile tea for the baby, and it can't hurt Mommy either.) Do whatever it takes to relax: Turn the ringer off the telephone, turn off the television as well, dim the lights, pull down the shades. You might suggest that people not visit you at that hour.

It's important not to be angry at your colicky baby or even to think that it is someone's fault. Your bundle of joy has only temporarily become a bundle of noise.

Crying is one of the things babies do best. The problem is the effect crying babies have on their parents. Some cries are unrelenting and you may be near crazy with frustration that you can't find a magic wand to wave it away. Cries can set off an earthquake of emotional feelings so that there are aftershocks of tension and despair which erupt over and over. Anthropologists assure us that crying is, in fact, necessary to keep us on the alert—especially at night when our ancestors really had something to fear out there in the dark. Some parents begin to fantasize real dangers during these dark "hours from hell." As in all natural things, remind yourself that these hours will pass. Don't ride out the crying storm all by yourself. Enlist help. Maybe your husband can stand behind you and massage your tense shoulders or rub your feet.

COMING ATTRACTIONS

If you have been using pacifiers, at about four to six months old the baby may start spitting them out. You can make the transition easier from using to not using pacifiers if you don't habitually stick a pacifier back in her mouth every time she cries. Pick her up and she may forget the pacifier. If your baby *continues* to need a pacifier after six months, which is not harmful, she is now old enough to put the pacifier in her own mouth. Throw a whole bunch into the crib and let her find one for herself; that's a whole lot easier than being beckoned every few minutes to "replug" a crying baby.

At about three months her cry will have more nuances and it may be easier to tell the difference between cries. You can more easily comfort your child from a distance—if you can't physically be there, your voice will often be soothing enough.

Most babies begin to develop the ability to comfort themselves—often by just cooing or playing with their fingers—and can hold off a bit on "instant" gratification. Learning to gain comfort from sucking his own hand, for example, helps your baby blur the distinction between your actually being there to comfort him and your not being there. You can also help your baby develop a transitional object (often called a "lovey"). Let's say you hold a soft cloth or blanket against you while you feed him. Your baby will associate that cloth with being held and he will learn the object is enough to bring him comfort. If you put that cloth into his crib, he may rub his face against it and be just fine without you for a while.

CHAPTER 8

Grooming

*W*hen your precious baby is handed over to you, loving him, even feeding him, seems natural. But you need to *learn* all the steps to keeping the baby well groomed. A little advice will go a long way. (And the irony of the situation is not lost on mothers who ask, "How can such a little person need so much attention?")

BABY'S HYGIENE

Mothers are eager to begin taking care of their babies: the first days home are governed by the specifics of *aftercare*. Wipe the base of the baby's umbilical cord stump with alcohol a few times a day and it will soon detach. It is best to wipe the cord using a soft cotton-tipped applicator soaked in rubbing alcohol so you can apply the alcohol where it's needed—at the very base of the umbilicus where it inserts into the body. If this is not done properly, the cord will get gooey, begin to ooze, possibly get infected, and be delayed in falling off. In some societies the cord is even saved for good luck or for medicinal use, though we generally just throw it away. Sponge-bathe the baby. You don't immerse the baby's body in water (and *never* ever the baby's head) until the cord stump has dried and fallen off, which usually occurs at about ten days.

Bathing

The first thing you should know about bathing is that it's a wonderful, ritualistic thing to do. When an adult is tense, we say, "Go take a warm bath." Bathing your baby, and even bathing *with* your baby, provides more than just an opportunity to clean the dirt off—in fact, babies don't really get all that dirty. It's a wonderful time to get close and for your baby to experience the sensation of skin-to-skin contact. It also provides an opportunity for you to see your baby's whole body and observe her in action. From bath time to bath time it may appear, for instance, that his fingers are a little longer or that his hair has more curl.

In general, you need to bathe the baby infrequently. I'd say it's safe to bathe her every other day and only twice a week in winter. Babies are often overbathed, and when they come into my office for their two-week checkup, they are dry and scaly. The only reasons to wash your baby are to wipe away old diaper ointment, if you are using any; feces; vaginal discharge; smegma from the end of the foreskin; and sweat in summer, especially in the folds of the neck, groin, and armpits.

I'm often asked, "When is the best time of day to bathe the baby?" It doesn't really matter. However, a colicky baby who is more likely to be irritable in the late evening seems to calm better after a warm bath in the evening. The traditional time for a bath is first thing in the morning—as if he were getting ready to go out and play and get dirty. It always surprises parents when I suggest they could bathe the baby at night, and use it as a time for you to both unwind. Bathing should be a wonderful experience which leaves both of you calmer.

The Bath

Newborns are very sensitive to temperature changes, and going from dry air to water can cause them great distress. Bathing can be very difficult at first, so ease the baby in gradually. It's a nice idea to start by just trickling the water over him so that he gets used to it little by little. (You know how most adults stick

Bathtime can be a wonderful opportunity to
include Daddy. Babies love the skin-to-skin
contact.

their toe in first when they go into the ocean. It's the same for
a baby, only you are sticking his toe in for him.) Some babies
hate baths because it causes them to be out of control of their
arms and legs, which often jerk while they are being held sus-
pended over a tub. Try holding your baby more firmly pressed
against your body as you trickle water over him and eventually
lower him into the bath. (Some babies don't like baths no
matter what you do!)

It's also a nice idea to bathe the baby while he's still on your
body, and with his skin touching you—maybe on your arm. Try
holding the baby football-style with his feet behind your elbow, again so that the baby doesn't lose contact with your
skin. Fathers are particularly adept at bathing a baby—they are
often equipped with big arms.

Use a baby bathtub, preferably one that is not too big but
allows about three to six inches on each side of the baby's body

—so he can move his arms around and not hit the hard sides and startle himself. Place a baby-body-sized sponge in the tub which can be removed after each bath and wring it out and then air-dry. Sponges that are permanently fixed to the bathtub are a bad choice, because you can't squeeze them out and mold can grow in them.

Most people think you bathe a baby like an adult, which means using a lot of soap. The truth is that babies need almost no soap at all. (They also don't need shampoo, despite the many shampoos marketed for newborns, so just rinse the head with water.) Use a droplet of any mild liquid soap with moisturizer in it—it doesn't have to be specifically designed for a baby. Remember, when you soap up your baby, the water you wash him off with is also full of soap, so he could end up with a rash. Lift the baby out of his little tub and dump the water. Find a safe spot to put him down on—maybe a towel on the floor—refill the tub with fresh water, place the baby back in, and rinse him off. (One mother solved the slippery baby problem by buying two tubs—one for soaping and the other for rinsing.) As an alternative, you could take a shower hose and attach it to the kitchen sink. After you have soaped up the baby, take the hand shower and gently rinse him. Babies usually love that.

In the first three months, a baby doesn't need tub toys. The baby needs you: sing, coo to him, or even take a bath together. Bathing with a baby on top of you is a wonderful experience, but some new mothers are still physically uncomfortable and have difficulty climbing in and out of the bathtub with a baby in their arms. I prefer two adults—one in the tub and one to hand the baby to. If you are alone, then put a baby seat outside the tub and use it to put the baby in while you get in and out. Never get out while holding the baby. If you do decide to take baby into the tub, remember that babies cannot swim or hold their breath, so don't ever let his head submerge. Bathing together is neither unhealthy nor unhygienic for your baby. It's actually quite delightful.

After the bath, unless the baby's skin is dry and flaky, you don't need any oils, lotions, or powders. (I find there's no place for powder in bathing or grooming baby. Talc can be inhaled by the baby and cause serious ailments to the lungs, and cornstarch can promote the growth of yeast in the creases if moisture gets in.) If your baby tends to be dry, then you might apply an alcohol-free water-based moisturizer after bathing. Remember, if *you* spent nine months submerged in a water environment, you too would get pretty dry-skinned shortly after emerging. By three to four weeks, some babies' skins have turned almost lizard-like. Your baby's skin may peel and flake especially at his wrists and ankles. Apply any water-based lotion a couple of times a day to these areas. (Warning: Don't put a moisturizer on your baby's face and take him out for a walk. That's the equivalent of buttering him up—you are literally frying your baby. Sunburning a baby's skin is very dangerous, particularly because the layers of skin are thin and the damage can be long-lasting.)

- Dry the baby thoroughly, especially in the creases—such as the armpits and behind the earlobes—areas which are chronically overlooked.

  (Note: I don't like cotton balls for anything to do with cleaning the baby. Cotton can leave wisps behind and make for a clumsy mess particularly when cleaning up a bowel movement. Use alcohol- and perfume-free wipes or a soft wet washcloth instead.)

- If the baby has a lot of hair, then towel-dry the head. This is a wonderful opportunity to give him a scalp message. With your hand supporting his neck, rub back and forth using a soft terry towel. Babies seem to like this and it increases the circulation to the scalp, which helps get rid of cradle cap. (Cradle cap is actually dead layers of skin and oil which pile up on the head, especially if you have repeatedly used shampoo and didn't quite get all the soap out.) Don't be afraid of the soft spot, which is actually pretty hard. I have found that some babies have cradle cap only *over* the soft spot because no one wanted to touch it, not even to clean or dry the area thoroughly. If he has a lot of hair, then comb it with a fine, firm baby comb, not a brush.

- Babies' eyes don't need direct cleaning, except if the baby has blocked tear ducts and mucus has gotten stuck in the inner corner. This is the only time you might use a wet cotton ball. (Ask your doctor to demonstrate this technique for you.) Again, *never* use a dry cotton ball, as it could irritate or cut the cornea.

Hygiene: Boys vs. Girls

There's not a big difference between washing boy and girl babies, but here are some tips:

- The vagina needs to be kept clean of stool. When you change your daughter's diaper, gently separate the external labia to see if there are any traces of stool. A white discharge is normally present, but if it is tinged with yellow, green, or brown, then it has stool mixed in with it, and the stool needs to be cleaned away. Otherwise the discharge belongs there as protection for the delicate skin of the vulva—so leave it alone.

- Boys who are not circumcised should *not* have their foreskin pulled back. If a boy is circumcised, use Vaseline (just after circumcision) to prevent the tender healing portion from rubbing against the surface of his diaper. On a circumcised boy, also make sure that nothing such as dirt, stool, or clothing is trapped around the head of the penis. (I recall one time when a clothing thread was accidentally wrapped around the tip. Ouch!)

Nails

Babies are born with long, thin, irregularly shaped transparent nails, and it's difficult even to see they are there. They may go all the way over the finger—like Rip Van Winkle's. The problem is that babies are also born with the reflex to clutch and grab, so they could scratch themselves. Even in the nursery we cuff babies with the sleeve of a nightshirt. It's tempting to peel the nails—sometimes they seem to peel by themselves, and when you see a nail half off, you might as well peel it. Don't use this as a routine method, because they do harden up within two weeks and can no longer easily be peeled without actually damaging the part of the nail that is still attached to the finger. Resist the urge to take your baby's finger in your mouth and bite off the nail—infection can spread from your mouth to the baby's skin.

Always use a miniclipper or baby nail scissor to cut nails. Many people find that their baby is resistant and pulls back. Wait until the baby is fully asleep and then cut the nails every two to three days in those first three weeks, because they do grow very fast. Parents occasionally cut the skin when cutting nails. The bleeding is usually easy to control, but if the bleeding doesn't stop within three minutes of holding beneath the cut area with pressure, then call your doctor. Otherwise, kiss it and just be more careful the next time. (Your baby may or may not be born with long toenails. If they get too long, then cut them as well.)

COMING ATTRACTIONS

After about six weeks, your baby is no longer considered a newborn and there will be many changes to mark the occasion. Your baby's skin should no longer be as dry. Nails are harder and more easily clipped, and they don't grow as fast. He is less likely to have cradle cap, and between two and three months the extra hair on his back and shoulders begins to fall off. In fact, a newborn with a lot of hair may start to go bald.

By two months, the baby is stronger, and more alert. You can expect your baby not to need his hand held to control his startle reflex when bathing, although you will still need to hold his head. (All of his newborn reflexes, in fact, are starting to fade.) He will lie comfortably in a half-inch of water and may like a more vigorous bath, but he still doesn't need a rubber duckie.

CHOOSING DIAPERS

After the baby is all cleaned up, he needs to be dressed. First he gets diapered. There are a lot of choices now. Some families are reverting to cloth diapers because of environmental concerns and the confusion of choosing among all the fashionable and expensive varieties of disposables. It is not clear whether you are actually helping or hurting the environment if you use a diaper service to pick up and launder your cloth diapers; you have to consider the gas it takes for the truck to come to your house and the detergent and hot water they use to clean the diapers. The benefits actually may not outweigh the potential environmental harm some people attach to the use of disposable diapers. Biodegradable versions are on the way!

There are advantages and disadvantages to both cloth and disposable diapers. Cloth diapers cost far less than disposables, and have the advantage of being soft and comfortable and are probably better for irritable babies. (Those are infants who cry easily—and will invariably cry at the ripping sound which occurs when you pull the closure tabs on disposables.)

Some babies have a sensitivity to paper and plastic, especially when ammonia, which is in urine, touches the skin. Also, cloth can be better in preventing the kind of rashes that result from an allergic reaction to the plastic or paper. You can't know until you try. The disadvantage of cloth is that the urine and stool don't have anywhere to go when they are in the cloth; it stays exactly where it was—against the skin. In general, most babies have fewer rashes in disposables.

If you use cloth and you don't use a service, you need to wash the diapers very thoroughly. Get a diaper clip, which holds the diaper in the toilet, and let the toilet flush most of the excrement out. (Don't let go, or you could wind up with a big plumbing bill!) Throw the diapers in a basin filled with a baby-soft detergent—but one which won't destroy the flame-retardant property—and soak them. Don't use a bleaching product: it will get the diapers beautifully white, but it leaves behind an ammonia residue which can lead to diaper rash. You could throw the diapers in a hot washing machine, which will kill bacteria so the diaper doesn't become a playground for germs. (If you have a backyard, it's still lovely to soap up, rinse, and throw diapers outdoors on a bush to dry, but not if you use pesticides.)

If you use disposables, you have many choices depending on your whim and the shape of your baby. Certain diapers are designed for babies with wide thighs, while others are for skinnier babies. Buy small packs and check out the shapes. Most disposables fit well enough no matter which you try. It really doesn't matter if you use so-called "boy" or "girl" diapers; it's mostly a clever marketing device. But look for ones that have resealable tabs—that's a really good perk, particularly when you need to open and close a diaper more than once.

Unless you are Tom Selleck in *Three Men and a Baby*, you will not have trouble diapering the baby. It's totally self-explanatory. If you use cloth, buy Velcro-tabbed plastic diaper covers to hold the diaper on—no more diaper pins.

Diapers should be changed whenever baby has stool. If your baby has sensitive skin and develops rashes easily—which you will know after the first week—you will have to change her more often, even when she is just wet. An advantage to disposables is that it keeps the urine farther from the baby's body. Often you can't even tell the diaper is wet until the baby has urinated about four times, because it soaks so deeply into the absorbent layers. That's great, because the layer that's closest to the skin remains dry.

The new ultraabsorbent versions of diapers have a special kind of gel inside which really does help absorb the feces and the urine. The pitfall is that when the gel gets very wet, it can come back through the diaper liner in small beads and get on the baby's skin. The gel has a tendency to turn a clay color when concentrated urine hits it. It doesn't really look like blood, but sometimes parents think that's just what it is. So I'll get a call, "There's blood in my baby's diaper." I ask if it's an "ultra" diaper and does it look red or actually more like clay or makeup? I explain what it is and we both breathe a sigh of relief.

Use a spray bottle of warm water for rinsing off feces and urine. The baby will enjoy the sensation. Use a soft baby wash cloth or a baby wipe for the finishing touches. Some of the newer wipes are alcohol- and perfume-free—they are costlier, but safer for your baby's skin.

Air-dry your baby's bottom or fan with your hand. (Some people have suggested using a blow dryer set on a very low setting, but there is a real danger of burning the baby.) Keep the diaper off for about two or three minutes so that air, which is the best drying agent, gets to the area. If your baby has very sensitive skin, apply a barrier such as petroleum jelly to her bottom; otherwise use nothing. Again, powder isn't necessary.

DIAPER RASH

Most babies experience diaper rash. It is usually marked by general redness, but the rash may be blotchy or spotty. The rash can spread up from the diaper area to the belly button or down onto the thighs and is usually worse in the creases. Diaper rash is caused by contact with urine and feces and is usually not painful to the baby, although it can be ugly to look at. However, if not treated, the rash could become raw and painful and even infected. Consult your pediatrician if the rash is bleeding, oozing, blistered, or if it gets worse after two or three days of care.

TREATING DIAPER RASH

- Change diapers frequently and leave the baby naked as much as possible.
- Rinse with water, preferably sprayed on; avoid using wipes; and never rub the area.
- Air-dry area.
- Apply a zinc-containing ointment liberally *to diaper*, and pat the diaper onto the skin.
- Apply an over-the-counter antifungal ointment if the rash persists longer than twenty-four hours. After forty-eight hours consult your pediatrician if not improved.

COMING ATTRACTIONS

When your baby approaches two months, the urine becomes more concentrated and is produced in larger volume. It's the same for stool. As a result, you have to change diapers more often. Most babies who get a diaper rash get it after two months.

CLOTHING

You should not spend a lot of money buying the layette. Often a close relative will offer to buy it for you. If you are doing the purchasing, let me *warn* you that you do not need the quantities suggested by the salesperson.

Even if you aren't paying for the layette, it should still be what you want. If you know the approximate size of your soon-to-be-born baby (and with sonograms you often can), that will facilitate shopping. A baby expected to be born over six pounds should have a layette made up mostly of three- to six-month sizes. The average baby is *not* "newborn" layette size.

Although you want to be practical, it's really a lot of fun to shop for baby clothes. In fact, the infant sections in stores are particularly appealing—baby clothes are designed to act as a magnet to attract you! If you find yourself drawn to a tiny Victorian dress or maybe a miniature tuxedo, smile and go for it.

Choose *cotton* fabrics—avoid all synthetics, polyester, acrylic, and even wool, which many babies are sensitive to. Yes, baby clothes come in uncomfortable fabrics because they are less expensive. They may also be less flame-retardant. They are not as comfortable as cotton, and tend to cause an allergic skin reaction, called contact dermatitis—which is an irritating rash of the skin.

All your baby really needs are undershirts, comfortable bed-clothes, and a few cute outfits for company. Unless you live in a very cool environment, you don't need blanket sleepers, which tend to keep in too much heat. (Also remember that for newborns there's really no difference between day and night, so a two-month-old doesn't need "nighttime" PJs.)

We tend to overdress babies. Rather than protecting them from the cold, this can cause fever, rash, and irritability. Think in terms of several thin layers. Babies don't maintain steady temperatures the way adults do. (I tell new mothers, who are often sweating—even in the winter—as a result of hormone swings, to use their husband as a thermometer and add just one more layer to the baby than what he is wearing. Preemies will need two layers.)

Shopping List

- Two dozen cotton cloth diapers—for spit-ups and to tuck in tightly under the baby's head in the crib. This is so you don't have to constantly launder all the bedding.
- Ten cotton undershirts. The simplest to put on are those that tie on the side. (Again, don't buy any in newborn size unless the baby weighs under six pounds.) Snaps are easy, but in the wash they tend to tear off and leave holes.
- One dozen nightgowns—*not* the ones which have draw-

strings on the bottom. If you buy or receive those, then take the cord out, because the little drawstring can get tangled in your baby's toes, legs, etc. Snap bottoms are okay if it's cold and you like your baby's feet to be covered. It's uncomfortable for him to be either too snug or lost in his clothes. Look for a size approximately three months ahead of your baby.

- Half-dozen one-piece stretch suits with snaps, not zippers because they can catch in the baby's skin. (European clothes often have zippers and are sized smaller than those made in the United States.) Be sure that the snaps go all the way down the legs so that it's easy to change diapers, and that the neck is wide enough to permit your baby's head to slide through without difficulty. (I've seen babies "trapped" in their clothes and squealing to get free.)
- Half-dozen cotton receiving blankets, which are warm, easy to wash, and stretchable—as opposed to the fuzzy flannel kind, which don't wear as well.
- Half-dozen absorbent terry-cloth bibs with stretchable necks that go over the head easily, but are absorbent enough to catch whatever drips down.

Also buy a plain cotton hat. Your baby's head comprises a great part of his body and he can lose a lot of heat through his head. Socks or booties are okay, but absolutely *no* shoes. (The very worst are booties or shoes made with plastic bottoms: they keep the moisture in and the air out, and even a baby can develop athlete's foot.) Your baby does not need shoes until at least nine or ten months when he begins to take his first steps and needs sidewalk protection.

COMING ATTRACTIONS

Your baby grows rapidly. Clothes can be as much as six months undersized—so don't buy too much adorable stuff in small sizes. (People often buy the wrong size, which explains why you will find resales of never-worn baby clothes in newborn sizes.) Buy for twelve months and up. As baby gets older, he needs more active wear. All clothing should be loose-fitting in order to provide for his new agility. He needs to be able to roll and stretch and move up in the world. Avoid doodads and sew-ons, which can be tugged off and swallowed by your little explorer.

CHAPTER 9

Enjoying Your Baby

It may seem as if all your baby does is eat, sleep, and cry and that most of your time is taken up in maintenance. The truth is there really is a lot of time to just enjoy your baby. The brass ring in the daily merry-go-round that is parenting is all those hours you spend *being* with and loving your baby. You not only have a newborn, but also have a brand-new friend—a buddy, a tiny partner in life.

OUTINGS

I often surprise new mothers when I tell them they can take their baby outdoors the first day after they get home. There is absolutely no medical reason not to. As long as the weather is comfortable enough for you, it's comfortable enough for your baby. Not only *can* you take the baby out, you should—it's good for both of you. The change of environment and air is stimulating. (It's been said that when you go out for a long time during the day, the baby sleeps better at night. I'm not convinced that's true, but it certainly won't make her sleep less well at night.)

There's also good evidence that changing your baby's environment gives her body the opportunity to regulate her thermostat. When you are in the same climate all the time, your immune system isn't as active as when your body is given a little challenge.

Think of these outings as part of mommy care as well. It is beneficial for both your physical and your psychological well-being. To start with, it helps clear your head—literally and figuratively. In addition, both you and your baby need sunshine, but with caution—more about *that* later. You can't get "rays" sitting indoors, and even on a not-so-sunny day, the sun is still out there. You are also getting exercise, you get to see and be seen, and you can show off your new status.

My advice to brand-new mothers is to get out even if you have to force yourself. Some mothers tell me they are too embarrassed to go out because of their appearance. (As one mother put it, "I look at the baby and say this is *so* right. Then I see *myself* in the mirror and think, 'God, I look so wrong.' ") It isn't always easy to get yourself "together" enough to be seen in public. (As another mom confessed at a new mothers' group: "It can be twelve-thirty in the afternoon and I didn't even wash my face yet.") The argument for not going out is that, by the time you do get it together, half the day is gone, or it's time to nurse again. The logistics of just leaving the house can be overwhelming. It really helps if you just relax and learn to go with the flow of your baby's schedule.

Don't expect to look exactly the way you did before you had the baby. Plan in advance what outfits you will wear when you go out. You don't want to waste time worrying about clothes—or staring into your closet hoping your prepregnancy clothes will magically grow bigger waistlines. If you can afford to, treat yourself. You can even let your fingers do the shopping and buy through mail-order catalogs.

WHERE TO GO/WHERE NOT TO GO

Plan and think about what you can do with your baby or just head out of the house without direction. This is one of the few times in your life when you can sit on a bench or blanket with

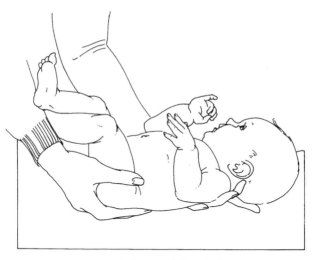

Enjoy giving your baby a "ride" and always remember to support the head and neck.

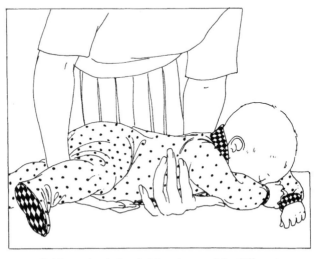

Babies enjoy being held and moved in different positions. This position may also help relieve gas or colic.

After nine long months, Daddy can enjoy taking a turn at carrying the baby. As the baby's head control improves, side carrying becomes more comfortable.

For variety, let your baby look outward at her new world. This position also lets you show her off a bit.

your baby and do nothing. Of course, you are doing something —you are learning how to enjoy your baby. (As one mom mused, "Once Jesse is up, I 'own' her for the day.")

• The park is one of the very best places to go, and not surprisingly mothers and babies are a common sight there. You will invariably meet other mothers, and you can exchange information or just smiles. Many lasting friendships have blossomed in parks, right alongside the flowers.

ADVICE FROM "PERFECT" STRANGERS

Becoming a parent serves as a rite of passage; when you pass through, it becomes perfectly acceptable to be spoken to and approached. As soon as a pregnant woman begins to show, she turns into a public person in every sense of the word. There is almost a community celebration surrounding you. I recall the first time my husband and I took our five-month-old son David out to eat. It was is if the entire restaurant had adopted him, and we weren't eating dinner alone anymore. Practically everyone offered to hold him, even though I was unwilling to let him go.

And we all know that "adoptive" parents also feel perfectly free to offer advice. When the baby is with you, the advice (which pregnant women are subjected to all the time) gets more specific. It may be unasked for, but it is not always unwelcome. Unfortunately the advice is often conflicting. For each person who admonishes you to zip up your baby because he's cold, another will come along to chide you that he's clearly overdressed.

Should you zip or unzip your baby just to please others? Obviously no one could, or should, follow all the advice of strangers. Mostly I recommend you smile, and thank the stranger for the suggestion. There's no reason to get defensive, to throw the baby out with the bathwater, so to speak, by discounting all advice. Try to see most advice for what it usually is: a way for strangers to strike up a friendship, however brief, with you and your child. The actual advice really doesn't matter. Children are perceived, by and large, as adorable and innocent. The child becomes the channel through which strangers can approach another adult. (Of course, it is never okay for strangers to put their hands on your baby, and you should stop anyone who does.)

Your world will instantly and spontaneously expand when you become a parent. Your child becomes an axle around which many new (and often quite wonderful) relationships are formed.

• Although many restaurants are hospitable to families, others practically "wish" you away. If you look in and spot crayons on the table or a children's menu in the window, you are in friendly territory. You will find that in the first few months, your baby should cooperate by sleeping a lot. The motion of your walking and strolling often makes them sleepy, so it's fairly easy to go out and stop at your local café for a cup of coffee. Again, most restaurants will be accommodating and you will quickly get to know which places put out a tiny welcome mat for babies and which don't (although you probably can't check your infant in the coat room the way Diane Keaton did in the movie *Baby Boom*).

• Shopping is usually not the best activity for you and your baby. Many stores won't even let you in with a carriage or a stroller. And unless you drive, shopping far from home becomes complicated, since buses and trains often require you to fold the stroller and carry the baby.

• There are movie theaters which specifically ban babies and cellular phones, because both can "go off" without warning. If you do take your baby to the movies (and no, it won't hurt her to "see" an R-rated one), be considerate enough to walk out if she starts to cry. For quick get-aways, sit in the last row on the aisle.

- One of the questions I am frequently asked is, "Who can I expose my baby to?" I advise you to limit the total number of contacts because of your baby's limited immunological response before three months of age, and particularly under two months. For that reason, I would avoid going where there will be large crowds or close quarters. In the excitement of being a new mother, you may wish to take advantage of all the activities you see advertised for families; but this is not the time for circuses, magic shows, museums, or even ball games unless you want to go for your own enjoyment. You will have plenty of opportunities later to take your child to all those magical events. We all enjoy sharing our children with others in the family, but whenever possible, go *out* to relatives because then *you*, can decide when to leave. In general, I would be wary of family birthday parties where there may be lots of toddlers around; remember, toddlers are particularly "infectious" little people.

- In warm climates, and in the summertime, beaches and pools are wonderful for *you*, but you have to be particularly careful with newborns because they burn very easily. Your baby should have a shade over her so she gets indirect and not direct sunlight, especially when the sun is strong. Use a PABA-free sunscreen specifically designed for babies, and apply generously to any baby parts which are uncovered. But a baby should not be spending enough time in the sun to get a tan at this age, let alone a sunburn. If there is a chance of considerable sunshine, make sure the baby is wearing a cotton cover-up, or consider not going out at all during the midday hours.

- Many public pools don't allow babies who are still in diapers to go into the water. Keep in mind that temperature regulation in newborns is not well developed. Even most community centers don't offer baby swimming classes until six months, because of the instability of baby's temperature. (A baby's temperature normally ranges from 97° to 100°F.) Heat flows from a hotter source to a cooler source, and when you put your baby into cool pool water, she can't regulate her temperature and she will lose her own heat to the pool. It's one thing to dribble a little water on her or run her toes through the ocean edge, but I would not take a newborn into the water. (If you *do* take baby into a pool, the water should be sufficiently chlorinated to kill bacteria; and always rinse your baby off with fresh warm water, because chlorine dries out the skin.)

GOING OUT

What to Take

I recommend that you leave a bag packed and ready for outings with your baby—it's the equivalent of a doctor's little black bag. If you are bottle-feeding and you use powder, measure some into a bottle so that all you have to do is add water from a water fountain or any restaurant. Even simpler: Buy a couple of nursette-size, ready-to-feed bottles; they last for months and months. (Check the expiration date.) Make sure you include plenty of diapers; wipes—or a wet washcloth in a Ziploc bag; a spit-up cloth; a change of clothes for the baby; and a plastic bag or two for wet clothes and dirty diapers. Replenish this bag whenever you come home.

Many of the new bags take the place of a pocketbook, and come with printed compartments. You can't lose things, such as your keys, because you simply attach them to the KEYS section. Tuck in some money, a small spray perfume, or lipstick if that's what makes you feel good. One mom confessed that whenever she passes herself in a store window and looks "bedraggled," she reaches for her brightest red lipstick. (I always carried a pair of earrings. If I went into a store or restaurant and felt I wanted to look a little special, I slipped them on. I suddenly felt different—more dressed up.)

As you venture out more often, you will know exactly what you need to put into that bag. For example, you might include baby sunscreen, a Vaseline type of lotion, and a magazine. (You can leave home *without* insect repellents, which work because of the specific toxins in them. Unfortunately they may also be toxic to little children.)

CARRYING YOUR BABY

- There's a whole variety of ways to take a baby out—from carriages to Snuglis, slings, and strollers. It's a matter of personal choice, but your baby's safety should always be first. Keep in mind, for example, that people can fall over a stroller and not even know it's there. To someone behind you, your stroller can simply look as if there is a hole in the crowd. I've heard mothers screaming, "Can't you see there is a baby down there?" If you really need to go to crowded events, such as baseball games, your baby belongs in a carrier on your body.

- If you use a carriage, put mosquito netting over it—not just to keep mosquitoes out, but human "pests" as well. (There will always be strangers who insist on peeking in and even touching your baby.) A word about carriages: Some beautiful new European ones are made with "windows." The baby can look out to see the world and you can see him through the sides. Babies are usually in the carriage for just a short time as a newborn, and by the time they can sit up and appreciate the passing landscape, they are usually too big for the carriage.

- You can carry your baby around in a portable bassinet. Even lighter-weight car seats, which are easily removable or have a snap-out section, can be used for walking around—as well as for riding in the car. If your baby is sleeping, you can just pick her up and bring her into the restaurant or wherever you are going.

- It's very popular to "wear" your baby. There are some

terrific carriers for newborns modeled on those of other cultures. Women have been wearing their babies since they have been having them. Even before we had the wheel, we had the sling—women wore their babies tied very snugly onto their backs, with the baby's head held steady with a big shawl. Nowadays there are wonderful slings which go across one shoulder that look like little hammocks. They can also be worn by fathers. In one version called Sara's Ride, the seat goes on your hip. It was originally designed for six-month-olds who could sit up, because it didn't provide back support, but now it's a whole miniature hammock. It's particularly good for people with back problems, because the weight is on the hip rather than on the shoulders. You and the baby's father should try on various carriers and see what feels right.

Snuglis, or front carriers, come in different shapes and sizes. Look for the convertible ones which adapt to different seasons. Some Snuglis are designed to let the arms and legs hang out. In addition to the traditional position of facing in, there is now one that allows for the baby to face *out*. I had a mom who always arrived with her infant on her chest facing outward. I'd say, "Hi, it's Mommy and 'Velcro' baby." It looked as if Jennifer were snapped onto her chest. Mommy would wave, and Jennifer would smile at me. It's particularly good for the two- or three-month-old baby, who can now look around and enjoys seeing more than just Mommy's blouse.

COMING ATTRACTIONS

One of the reasons I recommend you go out often now when your baby is a newborn is that once she is older, she will be aching to get out of the stroller. In general, she will not be so easy to tote around. You have about a six-month window, max, so keep it open. When you take a six-month-old baby out to a restaurant, for example, you will have to move just about everything on the table out of range. You may spend as much time watching and worrying as eating. (Sassy Seats, which hook up under the table, are not good until the child is fully sitting at about six months.)

By three months your baby will have fairly good head control so that the kind of apparatus you put him in can be more liberating. After three months you can even consider putting him in a backpack.

Anytime you are in a car he needs to be in a harness car seat, but it can face forward. If you are driving alone and can't put the baby in the seat next to you, which depends entirely on the kind of car seat you have, you can still view the baby by look-ing in the rearview mirror.

A three-month-old is more alert. He can grab at toys, and sit in a propped-up position. He will be awake for longer periods and can appreciate and swat at a little colorful bar across his stroller. He is still not ready for a three-ring circus, but now a stroll down the street is for more than just a breath of air. He can't wave, but people will wave at him. So continue to go to the park, and take him on picnics. The same rules apply to the beach, since his skin is still extremely sensitive.

Your baby's immune system is better at three months, so he can attend birthday parties and visit all the other places I pre-viously warned you against. He can even be exposed to multi-ple children without the same degree of paranoia you need for a child under two months. You can practically pass the baby around the table like a salt or pepper shaker!

ENJOYING YOUR BABY INDOORS

When you and your baby are staying in and he is awake, you can really put him anywhere you like. My favorite place is on a blanket on the floor. Until three months when some babies start rolling over, they can't get away. Although playpens have recently gotten a bad reputation, they are a fine, safe place as long as you don't use them as a jail. (If you leave a crying baby in a playpen, he really will feel like a little prisoner.) A playpen is just right, even for a newborn, as long as it's safety approved. That means there are no bars for him to get trapped in, and no internal hinges which could collapse. In fact, the earlier you start putting a baby into a playpen, the less difficulty you will have with occasional use of one later on.

You can also use an infant carrier or car seat inside the house. This double duty is especially helpful for those parents with limited living space. Baby paraphernalia does seem to take over almost like creeping vines. Jolly Jumpers are good at about three months, but walkers, *never*, especially if you have stairs. A walker may provide a fun time for your baby while he is in it, but it is not worth the potential risk. Walkers have been known to take babies places where no baby should be able to go!

You should be spending a lot of time being physically close to your newborn. Babies should come with PLEASE TOUCH signs. You can pick them up and hold them in a variety of positions that will be enjoyable and alleviate your occasional boredom.

There are at least four holds which can be used when your baby doesn't want to be put down:

1. *The Airplane Hold.* One hand is under the belly, legs sprawled apart over the crook of the arm, with your hand holding his face. To the initial horror of a mother in my new mothers' group, I took her baby and "flew" him up and down. He loved it. This hold usually calms a crying baby almost immediately.

2. *Variation on the Airplane.* Face your baby toward you, holding his head in your palm with his legs straddling the bend at the elbow. He is upright and you are holding his hand with him facing you; then you can raise him up and down.

3. *The Swing.* Sit on the edge of a chair with your legs apart, and hold the newborn under his armpits with your thumbs at the back of his neck. Swing him gently forward and back.

4. *The Traditional "Ride."* The baby is sitting up on your shoulders, wrapped over your head with your hands behind him—maybe looking in a mirror.

These holds are also good for *you*. If you can't get out, you can still exercise—weight-lift—with your baby as the weight.

You can also lie on your back and hold your baby under his armpits. His head may flop a little forward, but his neck will not break. (You really don't have to do that much head holding. The head does kind of "loll" over, and *looks* fragile, but notice that he is not crying.) Gently do "bench presses" by lifting your baby up and down.

A word about fathers: It's been well observed that fathers play differently with babies than mothers do. They are rougher. This doesn't mean that they hurt the baby, just that they give the baby a more rigorous workout. If your mate wants to spin around with the baby in the air, don't discourage him. Even if it looks scary to you, it's more important that it isn't scary to the baby. (It's a good time to snap pictures of him smiling with his father.) Fathers have instincts, too—they want to protect their precious baby as much as you do, they just do it differently.

INDOOR FUN

Babies really like to have their bodies touched and caressed. They are sensual and arousable—newborn baby boys occasionally get erections. We now know that touching babies is basic to their very survival. In one recent study premature babies who were massaged were ready to go home earlier than those who weren't.

It should go without saying that the more kisses you give the baby—at any and all times—the better. You may leave no spot unkissed. I've had mothers come in and say, "I feel it's not normal to kiss the baby below the belly button." If you feel

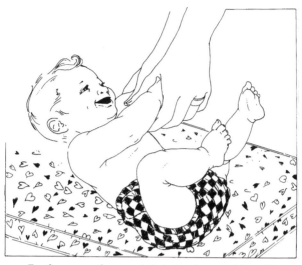

By three months your baby's head control is well
developed.

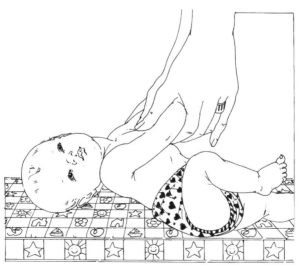

Play with your baby by gently lifting her shoulders,
but let her head rest on the surface until she is
older and her neck can support her head.

uncomfortable, then don't do it. But if you are comfortable, then don't let anybody else tell you it's not normal, for example, to kiss a baby's behind.

This is also a good time to go skin to skin with your baby. In simpler societies people don't wear a lot of clothes to begin with, and babies spend a lot of time on their parent's back or front. The sense of comfort and safety that these children have has been well observed. Being skin to skin adds to the development of trust and intimacy and is healthy, pleasurable, bonding behavior.

Baby Massage

A wonderful indoor activity is to give your baby a massage. If you can, set aside time every morning or evening. There are basically two kinds of massages: one is soothing and best done before a bath, a nap, or at bedtime; the other is more stimulating and appreciated after a nap when the baby is more alert. (In a soothing massage, she may well fall asleep if you put her on her belly.)

- You don't need to use lotion unless her skin is very dry, and then you can combine moisturizing with massaging.
- Put your baby down on her back and start with light strokes. Be aware, however, that some babies don't respond well to a very light touch—it's almost like tickling would be for an adult. Some babies prefer a firmer touch, even with gentle pressure. Maintain eye contact with her and speak softly or coo to her. Measure the response you get and respond in kind. Don't be afraid of the soft spot on her head. In fact, many babies will calm down when the top of the head is stroked.
- Babies are very flexible. You can take her toe and touch the top of her head with it. Gently, in a smooth and symmetrical way—first one side then the other, or both at the same time—move the baby's legs up and down or push the knees to one side. Think of your baby as an infinitely

more flexible version of yourself. You are exercising and massaging at the same time.

Bathtub Fun

I also encourage playing in the bathtub with your newborn after the cord has dried. In fact, one of the best activities on a dreary rainy day is to get into the bathtub with your baby. Remember, if there's no other adult around, put a baby seat outside the tub, lean over and put the baby in the seat, and then get out. (While you are in the bath, you could use a hand shower to gently spray water over the baby.)

TOYS AND NURSERIES

You want to ensure that your baby's transition from the uterus to the world is a peaceful one, so include in his environment the sounds, sights, and smells of gentle life.

Make sure that when they open their eyes, they aren't staring at a plain white world. Use lots of bright, contrasting colors. Interestingly, it's believed that black and white patterns are easiest for babies to look at because they provide the most contrast. It's not so much that they like black, per se, but black is as different from white as you can get. (You might want to throw a nice soft penguin or striped zebra into the crib.) If you buy a mobile, make sure it faces downward so your baby can see it.

Choose mobiles and stuffed animals which make soothing noises. There are specially designed teddy bears which duplicate uterine sounds and have been likened to an audible "pacifier." Lullabies are traditionally sung because they have a repetitive lilt to them. Your newborn is not ready yet for recording star Raffi—the Bruce Springsteen of the toddler set.

I'm often asked, "What does my newborn need to play with?" The answer is *you*. You are the greatest light and sound show in the world. Newborns need to be stimulated by living beings.

The newborn, up to about two months, does enjoy reflective objects, which let her see herself. The most fun toy you can give your baby is a mirror. I've seen cribs made with mirrors on the side—obviously they're not made of glass but a synthetic reflecting material. What's appropriate now are soft, plushy toys that have no small parts which can fall off and be swallowed. Again, choose bright or contrasting colors and materials that reflect in some way. There are even stuffed animals which have reflective mirrors on them.

COMING ATTRACTIONS

At first, the baby's reactions are to *you*: you are the toy. Before three months or so, if you throw a rattle into the crib, she may simply roll into it and wake up. She certainly can't hold it in her hand and shake it, though if you like you can hold the rattle over the baby and shake it for her.

At two months, toys can gradually change into action-reaction "teachers." She touches it and something happens: a light comes on, or a bell rings, or an object pops up. It should be very easy for baby to do. At the very beginning, the child will hit the toy by accident and then learn: "When I touch that shape, a bell rings." Eventually the playing will progress from random touching to a deliberate action. These toys not only are fun but make babies feel powerful—they allow them a way of interacting with the world. It's similar to when your baby first cried and learned that you come. Now he adds another valuable skill.

At three months, some parents begin to enroll their babies in gym programs. I'm a firm believer that they aren't necessary except as an opportunity for *you* to meet other moms. You can continue to be your child's own "Jane Fonda" by lifting and working out with her. As babies get older, they usually like to be massaged more. Your strokes can get stronger and can last for a longer period of time.

CHAPTER *10*

*Y*our *B*aby's *H*ealth: *W*ellness and *I*llness

*N*ew mothers often tell me that they worry about being responsible for another person's life. They are concerned that they will not always be able to tell if something is wrong. I remind them: You are not *alone* in taking care of this baby. You should be in partnership with your pediatrician. In addition to the standard series of visits, you are never more than a phone call away from the doctor. If at any time there is something about the baby that bothers you or makes you uncomfortable, call. (See page 167, "Calling Your Pediatrician.")

VISITS TO THE PEDIATRICIAN

Your regularly scheduled visits with the doctor—which are usually at two weeks of age and then at one-month intervals for the first year—are wonderful opportunities to ask your questions and reassure yourself that all is well.

The Two-Week Visit

- The main focus of this visit is to check the baby's progress and make sure she has regained her birth weight. Assuming she has, then the next visit will be one month later. At the two-week visit, and at each subsequent visit, you'll be told what your baby's length and head measurements are: for example, she may have grown about ½ inch in length and about ½ centimeter in head circumference.

(Note: Let's call this the case of the amazing shrinking baby. I've had mothers in my office wonder, "How did my baby shrink?" She didn't. Most babies are recorded at birth as being 20 inches; that's because it's difficult to measure accurately and the nurse often can only approximate the length. But you may go to your doctor's office for the first visit and think your baby has somehow shrunk!)

You will be asked to completely undress the baby—so make sure she is dressed in clothes that are easily removed. The entire visit should be full of information as the doctor examines your baby's body from top to bottom. Your doctor will explain, for example, that the eye color is changing, and the eyes are not yet in full focus.

• You and the pediatrician can really observe the baby together. Did the umbilical cord fall off completely or does it still need to be wiped with alcohol? Did the belly button heal well or does it need a little treatment? Is the circumcision healed? Are there rashes in her creases and folds—or maybe a dryness all over the skin? Does the baby's scalp need some attention to get rid of cradle cap?

• You may observe that the doctor knows how to calm your baby in a way which you might want to duplicate. For instance, when the doctor puts the otoscope in your baby's ears or the tongue depressor in her mouth, you may see that the doctor lets the baby wrap her fingers around his. The doctor may even put his finger, pad side up, into the baby's mouth for her to suck on so he can look into your baby's eyes with the ophthalmoscope. This is because a two-week-old baby will reflexively open her eyes while she is sucking. It's difficult, unpleasant, and unnecessary to pry a baby's eyes open to examine them, but as soon as sucking starts, the exam is easily accomplished.

- You may also notice that when your baby cries, the doctor may "cry" right back—in a slightly softer tone. Babies will sometimes stop crying to listen and will then respond in a slightly different tone. Your baby and doctor are communicating. You can try the same thing later: if she cries, just cry right back, but in a softer tone. (The doctor also knows that you can often stop a baby from crying just by getting very close to her. If you are within 6–12 inches of a baby, so she can see you clearly, she will enjoy looking at your face.)

The doctor will discuss feeding patterns and reassure you, or give additional advice on how feeding should proceed. You are most likely to hear that whatever you are doing you should keep on doing. If there's a need to change formula or switch to one with iron, he will tell you. He may ask you to start fluoride drops depending on whether there is already fluoride in your local water supply—and whether you use "ready-to-feed," powder, or concentrated formula to which you add water. You may leave the office with a prescription for vitamins with fluoride, or fluoride drops.

A common concern parents have is whether or not the baby is getting enough milk (particularly if you are breast-feeding). An easy way to tell if your baby is taking in enough is to check if she is producing urine and stool. (Because of the high absorbability of disposable diapers, you can't always tell if your baby has urinated. Put a tissue into the diaper and check later to see if it is wet.) The acid test, of course, is weight gain, but I strongly discourage using your bathroom scale. It's not accurate enough for "gram" differences, and you'll be getting an exact measure at this and subsequent visits.

Your baby may receive her first vaccine against hepatitis B at this visit. Your pediatrician will discuss this with you in detail.

VACCINE SCHEDULE—1ST YEAR

MONTH	1	2	3	4	5	6	7	8	10	12
DPT OPV		✓		✓		✓				
Hep.* B	✓	✓						✓		
HIB†			✓		✓		✓			
MMR‡										✓
TB test									✓	

* Third dose may be given anytime from 6 to 18 months after the first dose. The second dose is given 1 month after the first dose.
† May be given in combination with DTP at 2, 4, and 6 months.
‡ May be given between 12 and 15 months.

The Second Visit

Whereas at the first visit your baby may have appeared to be mostly passive, at this visit she is beginning to flower. At six weeks of age, she isn't quite a newborn. You have a whole different baby. The skin is not so flaky, and rashes and acne have mostly disappeared.

At *every* visit the baby's entire body will be checked. The eyes, ears, nose, mouth, neck, chest, heart, lungs, abdomen, hips, genitals, and extremities are all visually inspected and examined.

At six weeks you are able to discern your baby's habits and patterns—how long she sleeps and eats, when in the day she is most likely to cry. Parents often ask about their baby's feedings —maybe he appears gassy, or fitful after feeding. This frequently begins after the first two or three weeks of life, so it naturally comes up at this visit. "How do I get my baby to sleep through the night?" is a popular question. It's the doctor's job to give you the bad news: Most babies don't sleep through the night at this age.

At this visit you will undoubtedly want to know what your baby can *do*, understand, and see. The doctor will be checking out your baby developmentally—he should be making eye contact and smiling, and there may be some rudimentary cooing sounds. You and your baby may have forged deeper bonds because you can communicate more easily. Some babies now respond more readily to sound. Although they are less jittery (their startle reflex is fading), they are truly more alert—not just victims of their own delicate nervous system. They are, in fact, startled more easily by externals such as the sound of a fire engine or a vacuum cleaner. They may even wake up if you talk loudly.

The second hepatitis vaccine may be given at this visit.

The Two- to Three-Month Visit

At this visit, the doctor will be concentrating on developmental signs. The two- to three-month-old baby is significantly different in terms of motor skills than a newborn: she should establish eye contact deliberately; smile—and not just at anyone, but a special smile specifically for you; and she should be able to reach for and swat at things. Her grasp will be less reflexive and more deliberate: if you hold out a rattle, she should reach with her hand and get it. Some babies will even show signs of readiness to roll over, alerting you to baby-proof around the changing table. You can also expect her to look better: infantile rashes should be gone and her cradle cap all clear.

This visit culminates with vaccines against meningitis and polio. (The polio vaccine is usually given orally.) Sometimes there will be two vaccines injected at this visit—the second being the DPT or a combination of the two vaccines in one injection. The doctor usually gives these shots in the outer thigh and then hands the baby quickly back to you. It often happens so fast you won't see the shot, but you will know it has been administered when the baby wails.

DPT stands for diphtheria/pertussis/tetanus and is a vaccine which has an overstated reputation for having terrible side effects. The fact is that over 90 percent of all babies have no noticeable side effects from the DPT vaccine.

The pertussis portion, which is the usually named culprit in terms of side effects, prevents the disease commonly known as whooping cough; the usual vaccine side effects, if any, are very minor and are probably caused by the tetanus portion of the DPT vaccine—low-grade fever, irritability, swelling or tenderness at the site of injection.

(Note: Your doctor should give you detailed instructions on aftercare. If your child appears irritable, check the leg, and if it is swollen or red, apply a cool compress, and give a dose of fever-reducing medicine—an acetaminophen medicine such as Tylenol—which brings temperature down. The dose, determined by the baby's weight, will be recommended by your doctor. Some doctors suggest you give a dose of an acetaminophen *before* you come in for the visit, others give it in the office, and still others shortly after. It is very rare to have a serious reaction, and you cannot miss it. The doctor will tell you the warning signs. I advise all parents: Don't worry that something bad might happen and you wouldn't know it. You would and it usually won't.)

Let me make this very clear: This vaccine is required by law and is *not* dangerous. On the contrary, DPT has overwhelmingly saved lives. The mortality statistics since the introduction of the vaccine are amazing. As far as I'm concerned, there should be no controversy about its use. I have seen perfectly normal babies become desperately ill and in some cases die because they were not immunized. (There are, however, a few legitimate reasons not to be immunized with specific agents. If your child has a progressive neurological condition, or if a first-degree relative had a serious reaction to the pertussis vaccine, you must discuss this with your pediatrician at the very first visit.)

THE SICK BABY

You really become a parent at your child's first illness. Sometimes new moms will confide to me that they felt a little as if they had been playing house—dressing and feeding a doll. But the very first time you sense there could be something wrong with your baby, you are pushed over the fantasy threshold and right into the reality of being a parent. (As one woman put it, "I felt like I was play-acting, until Jesse got sick. Then I had to console him, and it connected that I was really a mother.") You may even panic and feel as if a hand had reached in and clutched your heart. It can also be very frustrating—you say to your crying baby, who looks as if she might be in pain, "Just tell Mommy where it hurts," and of course the baby can't!

WHEN YOUR BABY IS NOT QUITE "RIGHT"

There are several indicators that doctors use to determine if a baby is ill. If your baby feels warm, is irritable, and can't be calmed, or is sleeping excessively, she may be coming down with something and it's time to call your pediatrician. Poor appetite can also be a "lone" signal of illness. *Anytime* you think your baby is sick, call the doctor to discuss it.

Fever

If your baby feels warmer than usual, take her temperature with a rectal thermometer. Call the doctor if your newborn has a temperature over 100°F even if she seems fine.

Any baby *under two months* with a temperature *over 101°F* must be seen *immediately*. If your doctor is not available, then go to the emergency room of the nearest hospital. (Never give any medicine to your newborn without your doctor's specific instructions—not even Tylenol.)

When and How to Take Your Baby's Temperature

Do not take your baby's temperature unless you suspect she is sick. When you do, take it rectally, with the thermometer about a half inch into the rectum for at least one and a half minutes. The "fever strip" and other surface ways to take temperature are absolutely useless in babies, and worse, they often give misleading information. There is a wonderful new thermometer which reads the temperature via the ear opening, but it is not yet suitably sized for newborns. For now, use the old-fashioned rectal thermometer.

Don't decide whether your baby has a fever by feeling her head or fingers. Remember that her extremities and head are noticeably different in temperature from the actual "core" temperature. Her hands and feet should usually be cool. If, however, her hands and fingers are hot and you haven't over-dressed the baby, then you may want to take her temperature to be sure.

Before you take your baby's temperature, take off her clothes and let her lie uncovered at least three to five minutes. And no, she won't get a chill while she is undressed. The tempera-ture *outside* the baby doesn't influence wellness or illness. If you are taking her temperature, it's because you think she may already be sick and you need accurate information. (Note: Ba-bies under two weeks have very poor temperature regulation—you can inadvertently overdress them and "make a fever." You can also have a sick baby who doesn't register any fever.) So again, pay attention to her temperament.

Remember: Your baby's behavior is always the best indication of how well or sick she is. Never discount an irritable baby just because she has no fever. Call and discuss this with the baby's doctor.

COMMON ILLNESSES

The Common Cold. Many times parents will call reporting what looks and sounds like nasal congestion. Often it's not a cold but just the natural collection of mucus and secretions which all babies make. I get other calls indicating there is something different about the coughing and sneezing: "I know you told me that some coughing and sneezing is normal (in order to clear the airway), but she's coughing and sneezing more fre-quently and it sounds a little like her chest is rattling. When she sneezes, some yellow stuff is coming out of her nose." Those symptoms—in the absence of irritability or fever—alert me to give some simple advice.

The common cold is just that—common. It's less likely in the first two months because a baby still has transplacental immunity acquired from you—but not to the viruses you haven't had yet or that someone else is bringing into the house. If there is an older sibling around, it's quite possible he had a cold and passed it down to his little sister. (In fact, if you have an older child, your newborn may well be sicker more often and earlier than your first child ever was.) Fall and winter babies also get more colds than spring and summer babies, and get them at younger ages.

"CURING" THE COMMON COLD

- Your baby may respond to simple home remedies such as putting on a cool mist humidifier (which you must clean daily). The humidity provides thinning action on the thick mucus in the airways. It is easier for thin mucus to run out of the nose or even down the back of the throat and into the stomach, where it is harmless—as opposed to the lungs, where it isn't. It mostly provides some relief so that a baby can breathe easier and suck more comfortably. (Never use a hot vaporizer. It is dangerous; you can get burned and the hot water tends to encourage fungus and bacterial growth.)

- You can also "steam" the baby. Go into the bathroom, close the door, and turn the shower on to the hottest setting until the bathroom is much like a steam room. Sit with the baby in your arms or on your shoulder. You may need to open the door a bit if it feels too hot. In this case, the hot steam works better than cool mist to thin the mucus. Some parents worry that the baby will be all wet when she comes out. "Won't she catch cold?" No. She already has a cold. You don't get sick by being wet, and certainly you can dry her off before you leave the bathroom. Also, she doesn't have to be naked while in the steam.

- You are trying to help the baby clear her airways. You can't teach a newborn how to clear her throat or blow her nose, but your doctor may recommend you put some saline drops in her nose. That's a good idea. Others may suggest you elevate the head of the crib. That usually doesn't work—they just slide down to the bottom of the crib *with* their runny nose.

- Some parents try to suction the mucus out with a "bulb syringe" like the one used in the hospital at the birth. I find that very little is accomplished and most babies hate it!

- *Rashes.* If a baby has a rash which persists or looks raw, blistered, pus-filled, or bloody, call the doctor immediately. A faint rash often appears on the trunk or extremities in children who are ill. (Diaper rash is *not* an illness. See Chapter 8, "Grooming.") Describe the rash to your pediatrician as best you can.

- *Thrush.* Thrush is a very common yeast infection in the mouth. If the baby's mouth has a white coating which resembles Elmer's glue or milk, and it doesn't easily wipe away, it's probably thrush. It's usually on the tongue and on the inside of the lips and cheeks (the mucous membranes of the oral cavity). The yeast, candida, doesn't cause a fever, but can lead to significant discomfort while the baby is sucking, so he won't eat as well as usual. Anytime a baby isn't eating well, you should first check to see what is going on in his mouth. Call the doctor, who will probably prescribe an antifungal medicine, which is given by mouth. If *you* also have an itchy vaginal discharge, or if your nipples itch, you may need your own prescription or you may be advised to take some of the medicine prescribed for the baby and put it on your nipples.

- *Chicken Pox.* Yes, newborns can get chicken pox. You can't miss it, because it blisters with fluid inside. If your baby has been exposed to chicken pox and is under one week of age, call the doctor immediately. There is an injection which can be given to newborns who have been exposed to chicken pox. If your baby is over one week, the doctor may not recommend this, but still call and check. There is a new antiviral treatment called acyclovir that subdues the infection—but it must be taken very early in the illness. Newborns are known to either get an extremely severe or very mild version. The way to comfort a baby with chicken pox is to use cool baths, a calamine-type lotion, and Tylenol, if your doctor recommends it.

- *Allergic Reactions.* It's rare for a newborn to have allergies to food, because you are giving them only one food: milk. But if you've suddenly changed formulas, you could see a reaction. (Sometimes a formula goes on sale and moms assume it's okay to switch. It's not.) You could also see an allergic reaction in the baby if you've taken a drug, such as a cold tablet, and then nursed. An allergic reaction is distinctive-looking: it's not pinpoint or pimple-like. It looks like there is a "relief map" on the baby's skin and you can feel the edge of the irregularly shaped borders on his body. The rash—which is raised, warm, and itchy—changes before your eyes in location and size. A newborn can't scratch efficiently and may be writhing with irritability. That's worth an immediate call and visit to the doctor, who may prescribe an antihistamine even before you come in.

- *Vomiting and Diarrhea.* Most babies spit up. But parents will occasionally call and say, "It looks like gallons of liquid." (Of course, it's not gallons.) Sometimes it's described as projectile or shooting across the room. It's a larger quantity and has more force behind it. You may want to wait after the first vomit before you call the doctor. It could have just been the result of the position the baby was fed in—maybe a big air bubble got caught under some milk and forced its way up. If the baby vomits again, it's definitely time to call. It may mean the baby has an infection which is causing gastric upset or it could represent a "mechanical" problem—milk being unable to pass through into the lower intestines. The doctor will tell you more after examining the baby.

It can sometimes be hard to tell if your baby has diarrhea. Breast-fed babies have frequent, loose, watery stools. If stools have just gotten thinner, but are no more frequent, a little stomach upset may be the cause. You can help the baby by offering her some water, in addition to breast milk or formula, to compensate a little for her fluid loss. Vomiting in conjunction with loose stools warrants an *immediate* call to the doctor. (If at any time stool has blood in it, that's also an immediate call, although it's usually not serious. On occasion newborns may have a few tiny specks of blood in their stool as they adjust to formula or if stools are hard and scratch the anus on the way out.)

YOUR MEDICINE CABINET

Don't wait for the first illness to take a trip to the drugstore. You'll need to keep on hand:

- Saline nose drops
- A thermometer
- A fever reducer such as Tylenol for infants
- Syrup of ipecac
- A calamine-type lotion to soothe itches and sunburn
- A baby teething gel
- A nonalcohol, nonperfume-containing lotion for dry skin
- Alcohol
- Q-Tips
- Cotton
- Vaseline

Most medicines designed for babies come with droppers, which should be rinsed with water after each use. Never use a kitchen spoon to measure amounts.

AND WHAT IF . . . ?

In spite of loving and watching over your baby, bad things can still happen.

- You could drop the baby or he could just bang his head by *accident*. Calm yourself enough to notice what your baby's first reaction is: Did he cry, or did he look stunned and then cry, or did he stop breathing and then start to breathe again when you picked him up? Did she change color—if so, what color, red or blue? If your baby cries immediately on impact, that's a very good sign. If not, particularly if the baby passes out (or loses consciousness, even momentarily), take the baby right to the emergency room.

- As a result of an accident, your baby could be *bleeding*. Sometimes if you just turn sideways in a doorway the baby could "catch" his head. Don't be surprised if there is a lot of blood—especially if it involves the scalp. (There may also be a lot of blood when the baby cuts the "frenulum"—the little piece of skin that holds the lips onto the gums—and the little piece of skin which holds the tongue down.) Immediately apply pressure to the area that is bleeding, and *don't let go* for at least ten minutes. (Resist the temptation to "peak" at it. If it was bleeding badly and getting near to the point of clotting and you let go, it may start to bleed again.) Don't be afraid to press hard: I would rather you press too hard than not hard enough. If the bleeding stops, call your doctor to discuss what happened. If the bleeding *doesn't* stop, go to the emergency room.

- Sometimes while you are feeding the baby, particularly

with a bottle, the baby could get milk into her windpipe.
When that happens to adults, they gag and choke. Babies
are far less able to manage that; they can't sit themselves
up or assist themselves to help clear their airway. At that
moment the baby may look quite ill: he may be gagging,
milk may be coming out of his nose, his face may turn red
and then blue. As frightening as it appears, you must remind yourself that a baby cannot choke to death on milk.
You must remain calm and act swiftly. Look in the baby's
mouth and make sure that he is not gagging because the
nipple came off the bottle (if it did, pull it out). Turn him
over, hit him firmly across his back, blow in his face, and
hold him upright. He should start to cry and be just fine
in a matter of seconds. If he just doesn't quite seem right,
call the doctor. (If these gagging incidents occur frequently, even if they are brief, report them to your pediatrician.)

CALLING YOUR PEDIATRICIAN

You will have an ongoing relationship with your baby's doctor.
In addition to regular well visits, you will probably need to call
him periodically. The telephone can be a useful weapon in
fighting childhood illness. Every doctor practices over the
phone; we can diagnose and treat simple conditions. You
should expect your doctor to be readily available to you. In
fact, you may have chosen your pediatrician based on your
perception of his accessibility.

- Understand office etiquette. It is important to know just
  how your doctor's office operates. In most offices, it's the
  receptionist who is at the front line—but she should not
  be expected to answer any health-related questions. The
  most common reason to call is to set up an appointment
  or to find out if you need one. In my office, anyone who
  requests an appointment gets one. If there is a question

about whether you really need to bring your child in, talk directly to the doctor. Often I can make a suggestion or two and prevent an unnecessary visit.

- For obvious reasons, don't engage the receptionist in small talk, but you must be prepared to give pertinent information. Whenever you call—unless you are simply setting up an appointment—give your name and your child's name (today parents and children often go by different names), your child's age, a sentence or two about the major symptoms or problem, and the phone number where you can be reached.

- Find out if your pediatrician has a call-in hour—that is, a specific time period set aside every day just to answer nonemergency questions. I don't have one anymore. I found that only a limited number of calls could get through, leaving a parent waiting another twenty-three hours for the next opportunity.

- I instruct parents that when they call my office, they should "triage" themselves. You can't expect the office receptionist to understand the world of difference between relatively important, sort of important, and "can wait until tomorrow." If you say "this is an emergency" or "this is urgent," that's the verbal equivalent of calling 911. Most doctors will expect to hear about an accident—head injury, broken bones, bleeding, an ingestion; a child not breathing right; *very* high fever (the definition of which is age-dependent).

- Always trust your instincts. If you think something is wrong, you are probably right. Err on the side of caution. (When in doubt, it's worth checking out.) Call it parent's intuition, but no one is a better detective than you are at picking up the clues and cues—at reading the "flavor" of your child's mood or disposition.

- When you call after office hours are over, it should be a matter of some importance. If you call, you will invariably reach an answering service or an automated version of the same. Telephone operators have no training and often handle many clients at the same time. Try to leave a brief but specific message. Some doctors leave instructions with their service to be called only for emergencies and they call in for groups of messages only every few hours. (If it's not urgent, ask the operator what time the doctor is likely to call in for her calls so you will know when to expect to hear from your doctor.)

When the doctor returns your call, you might want to acknowledge the inconvenience or express your ambivalence. ("I really didn't know if I should call you but . . .") Doctors are accustomed to reassuring new parents, who are often not sure how to interpret and read their babies, who obviously can't speak for themselves. (I recently calmed a nursing mother who called at midnight because she noticed that she was rocking her baby underneath a smoke alarm which had a blinking red light. She couldn't wait until morning to be told that there was *no* danger that radiation was being emitted from that light.)

• Before any phone visit is completed, make sure you have all the information you need. It is helpful to organize your thoughts and write down your questions before you call.

COMING ATTRACTIONS

As your baby gets older, you will be taking him out more often and letting him interact with more people. At the same time, he will be slowly running out of your "borrowed" immunity and he will get more colds and run higher fevers. It's not unusual for a four-month-old to have a cold and a fever of 102°.

Your baby is also increasingly mobile. He will begin to roll over and put all sorts of things in his mouth. You will need to be extra vigilant, because your baby can get into more trouble. Clear the decks. Once they can crawl across the rug, at seven to ten months, they can put plant leaves in their mouth. And they do. (If you need to open his mouth fast, turn him facedown over your knee and squeeze where the jaw meets the ear, and his mouth will automatically open. Sweep his mouth with your finger.) Call the doctor, because the baby may have swallowed some resin from the plant. It's a good idea to know the names of all the plants in your house. There is a big difference if he munched on a begonia, which is safe, or a dieffenbachia, which isn't. Get rid of all poisonous plants. Always have the number for the poison control center handy. (In most states it's *POI-SONS.*)

PART IV:
THE EMERGING MOTHER

$$\bullet \; \bullet$$

The New Mother

At three months, you are standing on a threshold looking forward and backward at the same time. The paradox is that although the individual days may have seemed long (as one mom noted, "My days *were* longer because I rarely slept"), the weeks flew by.

It is both sweet and sad to say goodbye to your newborn. It seems that overnight, you went to bed with an infant and woke up with a baby. All the "coming attractions" we have been describing are now arriving! At three months your baby may sleep through the night, you may have decided to stop breast-feeding, and he is a much more active participant. In the next few months he will roll over and sit up, and continue to gurgle, coo, and "talk" to you.

The mothers of three-month-olds usually get great satisfaction from seeing themselves in comparison to their "newborn" counterparts. On occasion when a mother of a three-month-old attends a group with mothers of newborns, she is treated like a wise senior stateswoman. She is seen as having experience, confidence, competence. She's not so frazzled or worried about routines or daily care. At three months, mothers seem to have "systems" in place—whatever they are. And there's that incredible feeling when it all begins to work out. For one mom, that happened when Joey started sleeping through the night regularly and his dad began giving him the 6:30 A.M. feeding. That meant she had the luxury of eight hours of uninterrupted sleep.

Having workable systems in place doesn't mean there aren't still rough edges. As one mother put it, "I'm not quite the mom I pictured. I envisioned putting Max into a Snugli and taking him everywhere I wanted to go. It didn't work out that way." Some of that disappointment has time to bubble up to the surface, now that you are not so "possessed" by exhaustion. (It's always helpful to talk about these feelings with other mothers who have been there.)

Three months is also a naturally wonderful milestone for both you and your baby. Celebrate. Have an unbirthday party, take pictures, and compare them with the pictures you took in the hospital right after the birth. You were probably bloated and pale. You may notice that in many of your early "baby" pictures you have the baby "sitting" in front of you—as if you could hide behind a seven-pound infant.

THE NEW (PHYSICAL) MOTHER

You are not only stronger than when you first gave birth but less fragile mentally as well. (The mother-muddle fog should have lifted. As one mom joked, "When Jamie was a newborn, I had trouble addressing the thank-you notes. Sometimes I couldn't remember the towns people lived in.") Even to a casual observer, there is a noticeable difference. Often the mothers of three-month-olds will come bouncing into my office wearing eye makeup for the first time or maybe a new hairstyle. You are probably now dressing almost as well as your baby! You are no longer afraid to take the time to do more for yourself. You are gradually becoming a "renewed" mother.

There are physical changes *inside* as well—many triggered by your hormones.

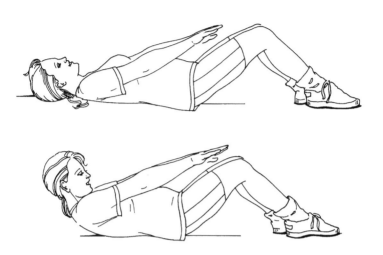

Modified sit-ups are a good way to regain your abdominal strength and tone. Keep your knees bent and the small of your back firmly pressed into the floor.

- There is a type of fat, called "brown fat," which is produced for the purposes of pregnancy. At three months this fat begins to involute whether or not you are actively trying to lose weight. (You could say your "baby" fat begins to just melt away!) This occurrence is linked to the changes in the percentages of your estrogen and progesterone levels—which stabilize by about three months.

- During pregnancy your abdominal muscles lengthened to accommodate your growing uterus. Now these same muscles get shorter. Unfortunately, the other muscles which stretched at the same time don't magically unstretch and *you* have to do the work by toning exercises.

- If you are still breast-feeding, your breasts will no longer appear swollen. The ducts have expanded enough so that you almost never have problems with engorgement. You may even feel that your breasts look "empty" but you are making milk.

- Dermatologists will tell you that most skin conditions will disappear at the end of three months whether or not you treated them. The warts, moles, patchy skin which suddenly appeared in pregnancy should all be gone. (Nature's "Clearasil," so to speak, kicks in to clear up hormonally triggered blemishes.) Those that aren't may be ready for removal by a dermatologist if they bother you. Hair loss has slowed and the texture should be back to what it used to be.

- By three months, your body has undone most of what pregnancy did, and you are recovered enough to get back to your prenatal state. That's why three months is the time when you can "naturally" get pregnant again. In societies which don't look to regulate birth, babies are often twelve to fourteen months apart.

MOVING OUT: EVOLUTION

You have nurtured yourself and your newborn into a new state. As your three-month-old changes physiologically and neurologically, she becomes a moving-*out* person. She even starts to *look* outward—to the world. She will try to sit up by arching her back. It's similar to the way you tentatively began to flex your muscles in order to rejoin the "real" world again. You have both emerged from the cocoon you needed to be in— now you are practically a butterfly, and yes, you will have to test your wings before you can fly back to all your previous relationships.

BACK TO SEX

In my new mothers' groups, one question that comes up over and over again is: "Am I ever going to have sex again?" The general refrain is one of exhaustion: "I'm just so tired." "Who has the energy?" "I don't want to waste my precious little time in bed having sex." The women admit to having thoughts as varied as: "Will it hurt?" "Will it feel the same?" "Will the baby wake up?" "Will I leak milk?" to "I'd rather spend the free time having coffee with a friend."

In a recent group a mother had just gone for her own one-month doctor's appointment—when she supposedly would get the green light to resume sexual relations. Her doctor asked her husband to wait outside and said, "You know your body is 'ready.'" The woman asked the doctor not to bring the subject up in front of her husband. (Later she hedged and told him, "Well, the doctor said I'll be ready in a few weeks.") This woman's story struck a responsive chord which resonated throughout the room. As another woman said, "All those magazine articles say that sex is a barometer of a normal marriage. If we don't have sex yet, does that mean we have an *abnormal* marriage?" Another woman burst out crying and confessed, "I don't think we are *ever* going to have sex again. I need to know, what's the longest time any normal couple has gone without sex?" She was panicked: "We'll never do it again and my husband will find another woman." Even though she was not interested in sex, she thought she had better be.

I've surveyed several new mothers' groups and almost no one in my groups is having sex more frequently than once or twice in the first three months. The sex drive does return, but it rarely "gallops" at the same speed as before. (These same women describe very active, romantic sex lives *before* the baby. As one woman said wryly, "We used to do it on the piano, on the couch, on the floor in the kitchen. Now we don't even do it on the bed.")

Tips
• Be comfortable with the fact that almost all new parents have to rediscover their sexual roles. (As new mother Susannah lamented on the television show *thirtysomething*, "Gary and I used to have sex. Now we have . . .

Emma.") Right after the baby is born, you will be fighting off the combined effects of fatigue and plummeting hormones. You can't go back to the sexual way you were, and certainly not overnight. I suggest to women that I wouldn't be surprised if your partner isn't really eager for sex just yet either. Maybe there's something hormonally protective about this. Remember, you probably don't want to get pregnant again now—your body is still depleted. (Babies who are born soon after a previous pregnancy are usually smaller and have the potential for a variety of related problems.)

- Seduce your husband only when and if you want to. When you are ready for sex, you could choose a date and not tell him in advance. Surprise him. You have the luxury of psyching yourself up all day, and if you change your mind, he won't be disappointed. (One woman who was not feeling totally comfortable with her body bought Day-Glo condoms so they could make love in the dark.) Often not resuming sex is simply a result of logistics. You may have to schedule close encounters of the sexual kind.
- You must be clear about *who* the couple is in the relationship. I talked to one mother about trying to recapture some of the romance and she said she felt as if she would be cheating on the baby. Yes, she has a "lover" of sorts, but he's six weeks old and wears a diaper. It is, in fact, normal to feel that your baby is a new love. It's not a perversion. You can feel pleasure, even arousal, while lying down and cuddling with your baby, or during breast-feeding. Your relationship with your baby does encroach on parts of you that were once reserved for your husband. It's helpful and healing to realize how universal these feelings are. They won't last forever.

BACK TO BEING A WIFE

The period right after birth is when the creation of a relationship with your baby is all-consuming. This is predictable and
natural. Some cavewoman first figured it out, and that's the
way it's always been. This intense bonding is for the protection
of babies. Call it Mother Nature herself rocking the cradle.

The overwhelming majority of couples choose to become
parents, and they don't consciously choose to damage their
relationship in the process. If anything, it's the love you shared
which propelled you to want to have a baby in the first place.
What many couples don't realize is that babies often act like
little earthquakes, rocking the marital boat and causing aftershocks which take time to subside. Most parents have no idea
how much their lives are going to change and they really are in
shock. When a relationship consists of just two people, they
usually have the time to be sensitive to each other's needs. But
add a child to that equation and the attention gets diverted.
Babies cry. Husbands usually don't, but that doesn't mean
they don't still have needs as well.

The ties which bind couples together can sometimes be
pried loose by little baby fingers. There *are* couples who do
unravel after the birth of a baby, but it's rarely because there is
not enough sex: it's often because there was little commitment
between them from the start. (Also, many new mothers harbor
deep resentment at new fathers who do almost nothing to help
around the house. As one mom reported: "Before the baby, we
shared chores. Now he says, 'You're home all day. *You* can do it
all.' ") Without ever consciously asking, "Who comes first?,"
some mothers treat their marriage as if the answer is: the baby.
Husbands come in a distant third in a contest they didn't
know they had entered. Their jealousy may be overt ("I want
to hug you and all you want to do is cuddle with the baby") or
covert ("Gee, honey, it doesn't look like you really need me
around, so I'll go out with the guys again").

While the child is an infant, no one should be asking who

comes first. Babies do. But there comes a point when the bonding has a directional pitch. When the baby is about three to six months old, the pitch should start to be *away* from the child. Many mothers start to feel a desire to reestablish their relationship with their husbands. The natural course is to yearn for the person with whom you made the baby in the first place.

There's a fine line to be walked here. I like to talk in my mothers' groups about what I've come to call "The Story of the Princess and the Bea." It's the story of the part-time working mom, and full-time princess, who jolted parents worldwide when she left her six-week-old infant daughter to join her prince for six weeks. While most of us commoners treat our firstborn like royalty, Sarah Ferguson, the Duchess of York, seemed to treat real-life Princess Beatrice rather "commonly." To answer her many critics, Fergie pleaded her case via Barbara Walters and American telly. As the princess explained, "After nine months of looking enormous and my poor husband had to look at me, it was his turn." The "poor husband" didn't have too many supporters in his courtyard. (Of course, we know now that this story didn't turn out "happily ever after" anyway!) While it's perfectly acceptable to assure your husband that he's important, leaving a six-week-old baby for six weeks generally receives the equivalent of thumbs down. Six weeks is just too early to decide your husband needs an exclusive turn.

But it is important not to turn away from your mate. Get reacquainted. There are circumstances pulling you apart, so you will have to work to pull yourself back together. Find time to be alone. Yes, go out for dinner. That may actually sound easier than it is. A mother in one of my new mothers' groups complained because her husband is insisting on taking her out for her birthday in a few weeks. She is already dripping with sweat and anxiety in anticipation. It's not just the question of who will watch the baby, but that for the moment, the mother would really rather spend her time home with her new daughter. Another mother in the group counseled: "I know it's hard to believe, but in a few weeks, you are going to feel different." By three months it should feel less wrenching to be away from your baby. You and your husband may find yourselves worlds apart on this issue—he is ready to take a three-week trip to Europe (without the baby) and you can't even manage a night out at the movies. Practice compromising now. Find a middle ground you can both live with.

LEAVING YOUR BABY HOME "ALONE"— BABYSITTERS, NANNIES, ETC.

Up to two or three months of age, many mothers really have no desire to be without their baby. (You may actually feel as if the baby is being ripped from you the first time you leave home without her.) You should be forcing yourself to go out (alone) for a walk, to get air without the baby attached to you, preferably by leaving the baby with your husband. Some new moms will leave the baby with their husband or mother, but that's about as far as the chain will stretch. And some moms have trouble leaving the baby with anyone at all. I have heard new fathers complain about their wives' "little obsession": "She doesn't even trust me with my own baby." Or, "She goes out to do a few errands and then runs home early to check up on me." Be careful what you do now or it could come back to haunt you later on. You don't want a child who can be comforted only by you. As one mother said, "It can choke you to always be the preferred parent."

Whether we talk about going out to dinner with your husband or even going back to work, the question is: Who do I leave this baby with? As one mother said recently, "I don't think I could ever trust anyone to take care of this baby. I love her so much, I can't imagine I would even have a good time—I would think that *she* wasn't having the best time. She can't possibly be as happy with someone else as she is with me." You have to let go of the notion that you can make this a perfectly comfortable world at all times for your baby.

The real issue is not the practical considerations—how do you find a sitter or a nanny, or how do you interview—but how you *feel* about leaving your baby in the hands of a "stranger." Tell yourself you are really doing this for your baby: you are slowly widening the "safety net" around her. This is just another way you help your child emerge as a safe person and learn how to "fend" for herself—albeit, a very little bit. I can hear you saying, "But the sitter won't hold the baby the way I do." That's right. "She won't smell like me." That's true too. Aren't you lucky that no one else *is* you. But it's not a favor for your baby not to learn other people's smell and touch. You will be back! (And you and your baby will experience the pleasure of your return.) It is good for both you and your baby to be apart on occasion. There *will* be times when you need a babysitter, even if right now you feel you will never want one.

You have to learn to be okay with the notion that your baby can like someone else. One mother had to get the flu to "let go" of Jenny. As she discovered, "I saw that she liked everyone —the babysitter, the housekeeper, my sister, everyone who came in to help out." For the moment Jenny is Miss Congeniality.

When you do use a babysitter, you can make the transition easier by leaving a T-shirt or nightgown, or any article of clothing which does, in fact, smell like you. You should also stay at home for a while with the babysitter the first few times. Let the "stranger" hold the baby facing toward you while she gets to gradually know the new smells and sounds and then slowly let the sitter turn the baby to face her. And always trust your instincts—if you think the baby really doesn't like a babysitter, find another one.

BACK TO WORK

The question of when, and if, you should go back to work has no one right answer. No matter what choice you make, you can't entirely "win."

The longest maternity leave most women can hope for is about three months. At that point women often have to go back to work or decide if they will take an unpaid leave and risk the possibility of never getting their job back.

In the past, many women raced right back to work—they are much less proud of that now. You rarely hear women bragging, "Oh, I worked on Friday, gave birth on Saturday, and was back at work bright and early Monday."

In making the decision, the first question usually is: "Do I *have* to go back to work?" If it is not essential to return quickly to work for financial or other reasons, many more women are choosing to stay home than previously did. It's become more acceptable to see mothering as the vital, important, and difficult "work" it is. You may still have to grapple with the feeling that you are not really *doing* anything. One mother who was annoyed with her husband asking, "What do you do all day?" prepared a memo outlining exactly what she did! (Keep a diary and you may be astonished at just how many activities your day encompasses.) The downside of staying home is that many women are still embarrassed to say that they don't "work." I tell mothers to answer the question for themselves this way: "Yes, I'm going back to work. I'm now working as a mother." Keep reminding yourself that you are very lucky to be able to have this opportunity—you are nurturing the future.

Many women go back to work because they have to. We are a two-paycheck society by necessity. As both a worker and a mother, you will struggle to find a balance. At home you will be thinking about work, and at work you will be daydreaming (or even "nightmaring") about your baby at home. You have one foot planted in each world and you will be torn. It's almost easier to justify working if you *have* to work. You can tell yourself, "I do the minimum, I will stay the minimum. Then I'm out of here and with my child."

Some new moms suddenly find that work, as fulfilling as it is, doesn't have quite the same importance as it once did. I just heard the "confession" of a dentist, a single mother, who said, "Work *was* once my major source of gratification. I still like what I do, I'm good at it, but I do it now more for the money." The income provides her with an environment she can enjoy with her daughter.

There are many women who go back to work because they love their jobs. Yes, they love their baby as well, but some women really need to get back to the "real" world—which for them is the world of work. Going back to work should always be viewed as a viable option, and I tell women not to feel guilty about their choice. It is definitely possible to be both a good mother and a good worker. Some women who really love their jobs are concerned about the economics of working. As one woman explained, "When I figure out all that it costs me to work, it hardly pays." That doesn't mean she shouldn't work. (A rather radical approach would be to "charge" half of the cost of day care to your husband's paycheck instead of considering that your check should cover 100 percent.)

WORKING IT OUT: WORKING

New moms who are returning to the work force are filled with the anxiety of practicality: How do I go back? When? Who will watch my child? (What if she needs me?) How will I juggle roles? How do I convince the people at work that I can still be productive without "killing" myself in the process?

You will have to make an effort on all fronts.

Make the transition back to work easier.

If you know you are going to return to the work force, then don't cut off all communications between your professional and personal life. Stay in contact so that people know you *are* coming back. Check in with coworkers occasionally and ask to have reports or newsletters sent home. If it feels right, then visit your office once *with* the baby—particularly if they made a big fuss before you left. You might want to visit one more time (without the baby) and check up on mail and paperwork. On your first day back, arrive early, as a businesswoman—not a mommy—although you will undoubtedly call home often. (And don't hang up too many baby pictures.)

If you have made the decision to go back to work, the one area where you don't compromise on is child care. You want to find someone who is wonderful in as many ways as possible: warm, loving, competent. You do not scrimp or cut back on quality child care. Period.

On the professional front . . . expect less of yourself. You are still a team player, but you may not be able to always go the extra yard. Even if you truly love your work, you may not continue on exactly the same track you left. (And you may find that others have figuratively placed you on the infamous "mommy track.") Work will not be the same, because you are not the same. Lay your cards out on the table now and there should be less hostility later. If you were known as the office workaholic, you will have to clearly state that you are no longer so "addicted." (Many women find that having a baby is an instant cure for workaholism!) Talk to your staff frankly and understand that delegating is an absolute *must*. Now when your boss comes in at five o'clock with a new project for you to do, you will just have to say, "I'll do it tomorrow." (If your sitter has to leave at six o'clock, you have no choice but to go home, or you may find yourself sitterless very quickly.) After a few months of full-time work, you may want to go to your boss and bring up the subject of part-time work. Don't assume the answer will be no. I tell my new mothers: "Let me plant a seed. Your company probably has no policy for taking you back on a part-time basis, but that doesn't mean you can't be the first." Many women today are negotiating a variety of flexible time arrangements. It's not perfect, of course. As one part-time lawyer admitted, "Look, they don't give me the important, meaty

This syringe style breast pump is one of the many
types now available. Start with a simple one and be
patient with yourself. The more often you pump
the more you'll produce.

cases, and I'm not going to be made partner, but the hours are
flexible, the job pays well, and it gives me benefits. And it
makes me really appreciate my son when I get home."

BREAST-FEEDING AND WORK

It *is* possible to continue to nurse even after you return to the work force.

- You can *express breast milk* at work, which will be
  fed to your child by the babysitter the next day.
  Go into the bathroom or close the office door, if
  you have the luxury of your own office. To save
  time, express milk with an electric or battery-op-
  erated breast pump. (Practice at home by ex-
  pressing milk between feeds. Don't be concerned
  if you don't express much milk at first. The more
  often you pump, the better the flow.) You will
  need a place to store the milk; if you refrigerate

it, you can use it up to forty-eight hours. Bring a cool pack to work to carry home the milk. (Don't put the milk in a freezer at work, because it will defrost on the way home and cannot be refrozen.)

- You can choose not to express milk at work and still *continue to nurse at home.* At work, again, find a bathroom and squirt off just enough milk to relieve the tenderness and pressure caused by the buildup of milk. *Don't* pump or you will just stimulate production of more breast milk. If you can, put cool compresses or ice packs on your breasts. It should take about a week for your body to figure out you are not "using" your breasts between the hours of nine and five. When you do get home, your baby will cry when hungry, and your milk should flow once again. Many mothers nurse only from about six in the evening to eight in the morning; the baby may even adapt to your shift and need only an additional one to three bottles during the day. (This method isn't foolproof! Some women come home from work tired and anxious and do not produce enough milk. I suggest these moms pump at work.)

- If you are planning to breast-feed, then *continue to drink a lot of liquid and bring breast pads to work for those* times when you leak. It's also important to make sure you have introduced formula to your baby at about one month. It can be harrowing if you try to introduce formula after three months—many babies reject it. (Even if you express breast milk at the office, you still need to leave a few backup bottles of formula, because you may not have pumped quite enough.) At home, instruct your sitter to initially feed the baby in her arms, holding a T-shirt or nightgown that *you* have worn while feeding.

(This position doesn't always work, because some babies over three months of age don't like to be "intimately" fed by someone else. Have the sitter put the baby in an infant seat and then feed the baby the bottle.)

On the home front . . . you are now part of the juggling generation. The trick is to see how many roles you can keep in the air at once without them all crashing down around you. Some simple advice: *Get great help*; balance the load with your mate; ease into the next working day by getting ready the night before; have a backup "pinch sitter" in place. It's been noted that the average working mother comes home to what has been called "the second shift"—cleaning, cooking, caring for the children. Decide early on that you can't be too concerned with the concept of "quality" time. How many parents come home after a full day's work and have *any* type of time for their children or—even less likely—for themselves? Yet they carry the additional burden of thinking that when they are home, the time with their children has to be the so-called "quality time." That can lead to what I call "frantic parenting": "Gee, I have only one hour with my baby, I better cram all the quality of the week into it." Quality time simply means making the most of every experience you do share. Slow down and enjoy the time you have.

Never forget that happy mothers raise happier babies. If you are always the giver and never on the receiving end of tender loving care, it can lead to depression and all sorts of self-abuse. I've seen many working women, particularly those who are in the "helping" professions, who don't take care of themselves. They are perpetually tired and never feel complete as a mother, a worker, or a woman. Women need to also give to themselves. (It's almost always the wife who pays the price for working when the psychological bill comes due.)

We all know at least one woman who does seem to "do it

all." This superwoman transforms from perfect mom to worker effortlessly. She always looks terrific and even manages to make cookies and Halloween costumes from scratch. We tend to imagine they are very happy—possibly, but not probably. You don't know what the actual costs are, because no one has manufactured a magic pill that replaces the need for sleep.

I counsel new mothers all the time: Don't look outward, look inward. Think of all that you have accomplished in three months and how far you and your baby have traveled since your journey began with your baby's first cry. You are, in fact, a pretty super woman already.

Epilogue: The Future

Three months ago you met a little stranger. You may have loved him on sight, but you didn't know him. Now you do. As one mother of a four-month-old said recently, "I can't even picture life without *this* face." These first months are a contained piece of time during which you are learning to become the mother you will be.

Although we've covered all the basics of baby care, you are still going to make mistakes. Even with information, it's normal to worry. We need to acknowledge just how anxiety-producing raising a baby can be. A mother recently rushed into my office because she was boiling bottles for five minutes and seemed to remember my saying something about "bottles breaking down." "Oh my God," she said, "have I hurt my baby?" Then she pulled the bottle out of her bag and the nipple was silicone, *not* polyvinyl. I said, "I don't care how long you boil silicone nipples. You sure don't have to, but they don't break down." Before I reassured her, there was palpable anxiety in the room. There will be many such "overboiling" occasions in parenting. And many more times when we can learn from each other.

It was from a parent that I relearned how to easily open the eyes of a baby. Early in my career I asked a mother to put eyedrops in her baby's eyes and I asked, "How did you manage

to pry her eyes open?" She said, "I discovered if I put my finger
in her mouth, her eyes opened wide." From that moment on I
shared that with all the other mothers in my practice. Mothers
are wonderful students and teachers rolled into one.

Raising babies is not an exact science—you can't cultivate
perfect babies the way you can grow prizewinning tomatoes.
It's worth repeating that you will learn by trial and lots of
errors, but it's important that you don't ever judge yourself too
harshly.

I watched once during a routine visit as a new mother con-
tinuously moved her daughter's fingers out of her mouth. Every time her daughter sucked on her fingers, Mom removed
them. I finally asked, "What worries you about that?" She replied, "I'm worried that she'll have an overbite." I sensed there
was more. Finally she answered, "I knew a young girl who always sucked on *her* fingers and *she* grew up to be clingy and
whiny." Another mom called, "My mother says I will psycho-
logically be damaging my three-week-old son if I continue to
kiss him on his lips." I call this *future fearing*—the mistaken
belief that if a mother doesn't do the right thing now for her
infant, or makes a mistake, there will be a wrong and irrevers-
ible outcome later on.

In one of my new mothers' groups a mother said that her
husband had recently read a study that suggested that by six
months a baby has learned all the sounds of his language. The
father misinterpreted that to mean that babies learn all *language* by six months and so he now reads to his son from the
dictionary every night. All the other mothers in the room
laughed. Our first inclination was to dismiss this as ridiculous.
On further thought, it was suggested that perhaps his dictionary reading was a male version of reading nursery rhymes and
singing lullabies. But there is a serious side to all of this. As the
mother said, "He is very upset if he misses a day." What the
mother also admitted to are similar feelings: "I'm worried that
if I don't provide the right atmosphere for him, he'll be bored
as a child and boring as an adult." What a burden to put on

the shoulders of parents. What many parents can't quite say out loud they say to themselves: "If I don't do the right thing now, my child will be a permanently messed-up human being." There is a lot of pressure on parents.

I always try to remove those future fears—you really have to stop believing that any one thing you do will have far-reaching ramifications later on.

The first three months are the launching pad which should propel you happily into the future. Remember when you came home from the hospital and said, "What do I do now?" The answer is, Enjoy your baby—your new, little, very best friend!

Index